Worlds within Worlds

Worlds within Worlds

THE NOVELS OF IVAN TURGENEV

Jane T. Costlow

PRINCETON UNIVERSITY PRESS

PRINCETON, NEW JERSEY

Library of Congress Cataloging-in-Publication Data

Costlow, Jane T. (Jane Tussey), 1955–
    Worlds within worlds : the novels of Ivan Turgenev /
Jane T. Costlow
    p.   cm.
    Includes bibliographical references.
    ISBN 0-691-06783-X (alk. paper)
    1. Turgenev, Ivan Sergeevich, 1818–1883—Criticism
and interpretation. I. Title.
PG3443.C66   1990
891.73'3—dc20   89-10733
                                             CIP

This book has been composed in Linotron Palatino

Princeton University Press books are printed on acid-free paper,
and meet the guidelines for permanence and durability of the
Committee on Production Guidelines for Book Longevity of the
Council on Library Resources

Printed in the United States of America by Princeton University
Press, Princeton, New Jersey
10 9 8 7 6 5 4 3 2 1

In memory of my mother,
Ann O'Rourk Costlow

CONTENTS

ACKNOWLEDGMENTS

There are numerous people to whom I would like to offer special thanks for their criticism and support during the years in which this book was written. First and foremost I would like to thank my dissertation adviser, Robert L. Jackson, whose admiration for Turgenev first inspired me to reread the Russian author's works with special care. William Mills Todd, Gary Saul Morson, Stephanie Sandler, and Judith Vowles each in their own way served as the best of readers for this project, giving generously of their insight and suggestions. Vladimir Markovich, my adviser at Leningrad State University, graciously helped to facilitate my year of research there. To my colleague Mary Rice go thanks for her review of my translations from the French.

Research for this book was funded by the Fulbright Foundation, and conducted in Soviet libraries under the auspices of the International Research and Exchanges Board (IREX). The Whiting Foundation generously funded a year of writing at the completion of my doctoral work at Yale.

I also acknowledge Editions Gallimard for permission to use Lamartine's "Le lac," published in *Oeuvres poétiques complètes de Lamartine* (Paris, 1963).

Finally, my deepest thanks to David Das, whose love and patience and sense of humor have made this book possible.

NOTE ON TRANSLATION AND TRANSLITERATION

The translations from foreign languages are my own, and have been done for this book, with exceptions noted in the text. Translations from Turgenev and from other Russian sources appear directly in my text; I refer to the Russian original only when necessary for clarity. In citing from other European languages I have given the original in the text, and my translation in footnotes. I have translated Lamartine's "Le lac" in prose, aiming at as literal a rendering as possible.

In transliterating Russian words I have followed two procedures: proper names and the names of literary characters have been transliterated in the manner most familiar to the English reader. Thus I have used Tolstoy, Chernyshevsky, Lavretsky, rather than their more scholarly equivalents. Phrases from the original Russian texts that I have chosen to reproduce in my discussion are transliterated according to the Library of Congress system, as are all bibliographic references.

Worlds within Worlds

INTRODUCTION

IN THE preface to the 1880 edition of his novels, Turgenev proclaimed what has become the accepted profession of his canonic realism:

> I have tried, to the extent of my strengths and ability, honorably and impartially to portray in appropriate types what Shakespeare called "the body and pressure of time," and that swiftly changing physiognomy of the cultured class of Russians, which has been the primary object of my observations.[1]

The terms and understanding of this statement of intention have served for many readers—both Turgenev's contemporaries and our own—as at once sufficient and definitive of Turgenev's aesthetic and accomplishment. The novels of Ivan Turgenev are defined in these words as "impartial portraits" of the nineteenth-century cultural elite of Russia: they are limited by the rhetoric of the author's own definition, a rhetoric that hinges on the writer's honor and impartiality, on a historical milieu that he "observes." The terms of Turgenev's own self-definition, it is worth noting, are shaped by the aesthetic of realism as he understood it: in observing and portraying impartially the life of his time, the author acts honorably. He achieves a goal both aesthetic and moral—ends that, by the time he wrote these words, Turgenev wanted very much to claim as his own.

The terms of this definition derive from the author's conscious understanding, and his acts of self-justification. They have, however, known a considerable longevity in the tradition of Turgenev criticism: the aura of moderation, objectivity, dispassion, and historical authenticity that the author himself claimed has informed the great majority of readings of his novels. Turgenev's much-defended claim of moderation has nonetheless come to pall the author, rather than defend him. Whether offered defensively or critically, definitions of Turgenev as a chronicler of his time embalm both author and novels in a shroud of naive referentiality. As the polemics they depict have receded into historical memory, the relevance and vitality of the novels have seemed to diminish. To assign to his novels merely documentary interest is to remove them from the realm of the literary.[2]

My intent in what follows is not to question the "realism" of Turgenev's four major novels, or their manifest concern with the social, intellectual, and political concerns of midcentury Russia as experienced—most often painfully—by sentient men and women. Too frequently those who would redeem Turgenev from a sociological indifference to art as art, have done so by wholesale denial of the historical, as, for instance, the Russian critic Gershenzon: for him it was a matter of indifference, "What the artist looks at: he will regardless perceive only himself, and will show us images of his soul."[3] To deny the historical is to deny Turgenev: it is in the complexion of history and the intimate, the life of society and his own lyrical perception, that Turgenev's brilliance lies. To celebrate his mysterious tales, or his love stories, while discarding his "social" novels is similarly to diminish him.[4]

The premise on which Turgenev's own profession of realism rests is, however, complicated by the novels themselves; novels that are conscious of aesthetic limitation and human ambiguity, that record the failures of human communication as well as the writer's efforts to overcome such failure. To know an author we must turn to his work, rather than to those critical statements he may have made about that work: the former will, no doubt, prove more complex, more ambiguous, more elusive; the latter hold no particular authority for our own reading.[5]

The novels' more profound awareness of limitation and ambiguity does not imply Turgenev's bad faith in his elder pronouncement; it does suggest, however, that the pres-

sures of societal polemic in nineteenth-century Russia—
and the prevailing rhetoric of literary understanding—necessarily restricted the ways in which Turgenev's novels
could be understood. Nineteenth-century Russian critics
were not interested in enigmas; they were interested in so-
lutions. Twentieth-century Western critics have in turn
been less interested in Turgenev's understated aesthetic,
more enthralled by the maximalism and "Russianness" of
Dostoevsky and Tolstoy.[6]

The following chapters attempt to some extent to account for both the historicity and the aesthetic elegance of
Turgenev's novels: like the simplest painting of our daily
artifacts, these works please in part because they shape a
world we recognize. Our pleasure is in the form as in the
content, in the form that gives to the formed its resonant
signifying power. The fundamental impulse of this book is
nonetheless to treat Turgenev's four major novels in literary, rather than historical terms, to accept the complexity
and subtlety those novels possess, and to articulate the
meanings they embody. In a very basic sense, my readings, while they do allude to history—both literary and social—do not originate within the historical; they originate
within Turgenev's texts, which in their capacity to com-
municate beyond their moment and context of utterance
manifest a principle of rejuvenation and contemporaneity
that defines them as literary.[7]

The direction my own discussion will take is to a certain
extent suggested in another "reading" of Turgenev, from
which the title of this book is taken. Writing to his brother
Henry in June of 1876, William James articulated his admiration of Turgenev in language that is suggestive for my
own ends. "It is the amount of life which a man feels that
makes you value his mind, and Turgueneff has a sense of
worlds within worlds whose existence is unsuspected by
the vulgar."[8] James's terms are curious, and intriguing: he
implies that we value mind only in connection with feeling; that thought and feeling in a particular balance make
possible the perception (or "sensing") of that which is nor-

mally unapparent. James's terms, in fact, come back to Turgenev's own 1880 statement, culminating as they do in the issue of perception (Turgenev's "the primary object of my observations"). But the nature of literary genesis and relationship as James articulates it differs significantly from Turgenev's statement, and it is James who more closely touches on the particularity of Turgenev's novels that these essays seek to elucidate.

The turn of phrase most striking in James's praise is that which defines the topography of Turgenev's perception: "Turgenev has a sense of worlds within worlds unsuspected by the vulgar." Sentience in such terms might become an agent of elite hermeticism, defending the artist from "the vulgar." In the light of Turgenev's major novels the words nonetheless have a very different, even opposite, significance: it is the meek and powerless of Turgenev's world who are more often blessed with the gift of perception. It is the topography itself, however, that is most significant—the topography of the world Turgenev has perceived and portrayed.

James's terms point to an opposition of appearance and being, of the social and the intimate, which is narrated in Turgenev's major novels; those terms also suggest an opposition grounded in our own reading, of "surface" meaning and problematic depth, an opposition I will recall in my treatment of Turgenev's narrative. I understand James's terms, then, as pointing both to Turgenev's activity and to ours as readers. The "object" of Turgenev's "observations" is more often than not the unseen dramas that occur within society. His own manner of seeing them privileges the unseen as much as it does the communal. As readers, we must be attentive to the oblique and hidden senses of Turgenev's prose. As one of our finest contemporary critics has put it, "Although [narrative's] function is mnemonic, it always recalls different things."[9] What I want to attend to is some of those "different things" to which Turgenev's narrative refers.

The coexistence of realms in Turgenev's narrative topography is sometimes architectural, as in *A Nest of Gentry*, where the gentry world is split into an upper and lower realm that represent truth and gossip, spirit and hypocrisy. In other cases it is more oblique, as when Turgenev's lyric narrator shapes a social novel with a vision and voice that is private and hidden from the eyes of the "vulgar" within the narrative itself. Or the worlds within worlds may refer to genre itself: as when Turgenev places within the social novel a pastoral realm that functions as an imaginative world through which Turgenev projects his understanding and aspirations. What we gain by attending to Turgenev's novels in this way is a sense of their complex interweaving of history and the lyrical, of Turgenev's modification of the social novel by his own poetic vision and meditative concerns. Within the world of history and the narrative that records it, there exists another realm: of lyric meditation, pastoral rejuvenation, unspoken emotion. These are the realms that the following chapters will explore in some detail; it is in them that I find the particular qualities of Turgenev's narrative.

My intention is to take James's words as a guide for my own activity as reader. I will suggest a way of looking at the worlds within Turgenev's novels that accepts this topography of the seen and unseen. Chapter 1 serves as groundwork for much of what follows, in its discussion of aspects of Turgenev's use of language, dialogue, and gesture: Turgenev's first novel, *Rudin*, and his story, "Journey into the Woodland," both trace an evolution that was the author's own, from inflated romantic rhetoric to the "simplicities" of prose. I nonetheless suggest that the enigmas and hiddenness of Turgenev's early poetry linger in his later work, as a residue of lyricism that fundamentally affects the way we read him. Chapters 2 and 3 are devoted to *A Nest of Gentry*. In chapter 2 I examine the counterpoint of salon discourse and silence in the novel. In chapter 3 I focus more on the novel as a narrative polemic with Slavophile historiography—a polemic conducted not primarily in salon dispute, but in the very shaping of the plot. In chapter 4 I again examine the problem of lyrical elements in the Turgenevan novel—in this instance, the problem of how the concerns of a specific subtext counter, and ultimately subvert, heroic plot in *On the Eve*. Chapter 5 deals with *Fathers and Children*, and considers that novel's concern with passional human existence: the political problematic of the novel is grounded, I argue, in Turgenev's darker perceptions of human sexuality, perceptions that inform both his political psychology and his aesthetics.

These chapters are all unabashed essays in close reading: I work toward understandings of Turgenev's aesthetics, of the ways in which his political and psychological convictions inform his artistic choices, by moving slowly through the subtleties and enigmas of his texts. Many of our received opinions about Turgenev are thus "tabled"; my intent is not to take on those opinions (though I periodically refer to divergent readings in my notes), but to attempt to open up Turgenev's works once again, to argue that they are, in all their apparent simplicity, enigmatic and challenging. One of my central suggestions throughout these essays is that the paradox of simplicity and enigma forms the pivot of Turgenev's poetics, that his elegant surfaces mask problematic depths.

These essays constitute attempts to read Turgenev anew, to discover in the reading how one should read him. Turgenev himself offers scenarios of reading in these works, scenarios that I take as suggestions for our own activity. In *A Nest of Gentry*, the boy Lavretsky sits with a book of Baroque Emblems whose pictures and words resist his understanding. The figures depicted are both conventional and familiar—but the relationship between those figures and the accompanying messages is unclear. Two familiar and apparently unambiguous elements become, when combined, enigmatic and perplexing. In the narrative of Lavretsky's life, the reading of this book is significant: it draws him out of a world of darkness, but cannot prevent his fatal mistakes of judgment. The enigmas of the Book of Emblems are comprehensible to him—as to us—only in the larger context of his story. The figures do not help Lavretsky in his life—but his life does suggest a possible reading of the emblems.

This scene of reading, which mixes imagination and perplexity, emancipation and defeat, had autobiographical significance for Turgenev, whose childhood reading included the baroque volume. The scene is central in Turgenev's narratives, however, because it suggests tensions and possibilities in the reading of his own texts. One can plausibly read this passage as a suggestion of the prominence of emblems in Turgenev's own prose, of his use of observed details that create a known world but have more enigmatic meaning as well. The passage also suggests an understanding of reading as an activity that is at once laden with potential and doomed to failure, or at least to incompletion. Readings of Turgenev have too often in the past accepted a lesser challenge: to find the historical referents of his characters, his plots, his authorial allegiances; to assimilate the meanings of his narratives to his extratextual proclamations. Lavretsky's reading, on the other hand, is neither so useful nor so bound. The movement of imagination here is to some extent free—tempered by plot and linearity, but also capable of play and unfettered movement. The movement of imagination and memory in *A Nest of Gentry* is also the movement of Turgenev's prose: his language edges forward, to tell a tale, but it also returns upon itself, to form the symmetries and repetitions of lyric intention.

The progress of these essays is from a focus on Turgenev's language—in his first novel, *Rudin*—to an examination of the relationship between his use of a specific literary genre and his political convictions, in *Fathers and Children*. Broadly speaking I move from a focus on language to a focus on history. For Turgenev, however, the two concerns are essentially indivisible: all of his novels are concerned with the fate of Russia, with the realization of justice in a homeland he both loved and hated. The subtleties of Turgenev's novelistic skill and the tendency of his lyrical gift to qualify illusory longings are always directed toward this larger project: the knowledge of self necessary to both individuals and nations if they are to succeed in the living of a free life.

Chapter One

RHETORIC AND SINCERITY: TURGENEV AND THE POETICS OF SILENCE

ALL OF Turgenev's novels are, to a very large extent, novels of polite conversation, where the narrative's progress is marked less by event than by the nuance of verbal exchange and encounter. The Soviet scholar L. V. Pumpiansky, in an article of 1940 whose terminology has been often repeated, defined Turgenev's novels as "personal novels about culture"—in distinction to the "novels of event" associated with Balzac.[1]

Turgenev's disdain for the complex, melodramatic plotting of authors like Dumas is unequivocal in his 1852 review of Evgeniya Tur's novel, *The Niece*: "Novels *à la Dumas* with numbers of volumes *ad libidum* certainly exist in our country; but the reader will permit us to pass over them in silence. They may well be a fact, but not all facts have significance" (V, 373). Turgenev's own sense of the possibilities open to the Russian novel is evident in this review in his naming of two existing narrative types: those associated with Charles Dickens and with George Sand. Turgenev qualifies his enumeration of possibilities by questioning whether Russia is yet sufficiently "pronounced" as a society to permit four-volume novels; his implication is that the unformed nature of Russian society calls for fragmentary narrative: "Are the elements of our society's life sufficiently pronounced to expect four volumes from the novel that attempts to depict them? The most recent success of various sketches seems to prove the opposite. As yet we are hearing separate sounds from Russian life, which poetry answers with equally rapid echoes" (V, 373).

My intent here is not to address the problem of the narrative precursors and sources of the Turgenev novel—though it does appear to me an interesting problem, and one as yet incompletely answered. The sources of Turgenev's own novelistic form lie both in existing narrative traditions, and in the drama, a form in which he worked throughout the 1840s and into the early 1850s, until his full-length play, "A Month in the Country," met with disapproval and critical misperception in the 1850s.[2] What is of interest to me here is the fact that Turgenev elaborates a novelistic form that depends less on the complexities of plot than on the revelations of conversation—and his first novel, *Rudin*, is in this regard a crucial guide to what conversation in Turgenev is all about. Turgenev's first exercise in that larger form he both sought and feared is a novel *about* talk—about rhetoric, truth, sincerity, significance—and as such suggests the aesthetic that will inform all of his work.

The historical and biographical impetus for this novel's concerns lies in that period of Russia's intellectual life that *Rudin* to some extent depicts: the connection of Turgenev's fictional hero with the anarchist Bakunin, the representation in Pokorsky of N. Stankevich, an intellectual mentor idolized after his early death, the depiction of the atmosphere of Moscow's philosophical circles of the late 1830s—all of these historical referents have been extensively documented.[3] What is striking about Turgenev's novel, however, is its translation of the agonies and ideas of his generation into a novel that, in criticizing the rhetoric and philosophizing of its hero, finds other ways of articulating life's significance. Turgenev's translation of his generation's concerns is ultimately a subversion—not merely of Bakunin/Rudin, but of philosophy per se, and of the pretensions of philosophical discourse. Turgenev's novel is a protracted act of disengagement from an intellectual milieu that had possessed him—and in its movement from philosophy to narrative the novel traces an evolution that was Turgenev's own.[4]

The evolution that I will trace in these pages is one enacted in several works of Turgenev's early years as a novelist. The passages of Turgenev himself as he moved toward the novel as a genre are complex, and should not be overlooked in considering the forms his later narrative took. The transition from the fragmentary form of *The Huntsman's Sketches* to the longer form of the novel was of great moment to Turgenev himself: he struggled with longer narrative, doubted his abilities in his first effort (*Two Generations*, which he destroyed), and wavered throughout his career in knowing just how to name his longer prose: novellas or novels.[5] The passages I will trace here, however, have less to do with length than with language, and with the author's efforts to distance himself from the rhetoric and effusions of his youth. *Rudin*, Turgenev's first novel; "Journey into the Woodland," a novella of 1857; and "Diary of a Superfluous Man," of 1850, all concern themselves with the problematics of revelation, consciousness, and speech. *Rudin* is most directly linked to the excesses and pretentious rhetoric of German Idealism in Russia, and is hence most specifically grounded in the cultural moment of Turgenev's youth. "Journey into the Woodland" alludes to another of Turgenev's youthful enthusiasms, his early lyric poetry; its narrative traces the author's movement beyond what seemed to him imitative solipsism.[6] All three works, however, articulate an understanding of narrative's specific possibilities that is crucial in our reading of Turgenev. What he articulates, in these works, is a way of understanding what is "significant," an understanding that is characteristically grounded in the tension between worlds: of consciousness and simplicity, rhetoric and silence, solipsism and sincerity. The rhetoric—and rhetoricians—of significance fade in Turgenev's narrative (as in his life) before the nuance of gesture, hiddenness, and the everyday. These narratives hold something of a privileged place in Turgenev's oeuvre: they establish how he will construe narrative meaning, and point to how we must read it.

Turgenev returns to philosophy and poetry in his novels, but in a form radically understated and oblique, with none of the pretensions of his early selves. He continues to be read as a "novelist of ideas," as an admirer of men who embody ideas and ideals.[7] Such readings are not wrong, but they do need serious qualification, for in many cases the "defeat" of the hero at the hands of reality implies a defeat of ideas as well, and an affirmation of the medial and immediate existence the hero has challenged. What survives Turgenev's heroic ideologues—and both Rudin and Bazarov are his most explicitly ideological figures—is not banality but an everyday existence that holds to a balance which those heroes disdain. Turgenev is in no way blind to the miseries and stupidities of Russian reality—but his narratives evoke a daily simplicity and fullness that breaks with the Gogolian. It is these visions of everyday life—of everyday language and measured labor—that are Turgenev's ideals.

Writing of Turgenev's early narrative poem "Parasha," Waclaw Lednicki has suggested both its debt to, and distance from, Pushkin's *Eugene Onegin*, in precisely this realm: the everyday. "Turgenev marries his hero to Parasha and commands them to attain the goal of 'everyday happiness,' which was not reached by Onegin and Tatyana, nor by Lensky. . . . The bourgeois happiness from which Pushkin saved Lensky became the fate of Turgenev's heroes."[8] To call such happiness a "fate" from which others are "saved" suggests doom and desolation; I will suggest the opposite—that it is this "everyday happiness" that Turgenev evokes as ideal in *Rudin*, and that such happiness for Turgenev involves breaking with notions of heroism, epiphany, and absolutes.

In a letter of 1860 to Evgeniya Lambert, Turgenev described a departure from St. Petersburg that was also a return to a "well-lived life": "And I'm glad to get rested after a worrisome Petersburg winter—to live for a while a normal life, with a small dose of quiet boredom—that true sign of the proper passing of time" (P, IV, 90). The well-

lived life, the life of "quiet boredom," is what remains after satire and heroism in Turgenev's novels; it has its civic
counterpart in Turgenev's "English" liberalism, his commitment to evolution, his despair at the increasing alienation of late nineteenth-century politics. The language of
Turgenev's novels is the language of that well-lived life, a
language of understatement and modesty, a language that
avoids confession, gossip, and revelation. There is, of
course, lots of gossip in Turgenev's novels—in both *Rudin*
and *A Nest of Gentry* and in the later *Smoke*—just as there
is much revelation and confession in *Rudin*. But what is
important to note is that these ways of speaking are dis-
tanced and displaced by Turgenev, that he is critical of his
characters for the ways in which they use words. It is this
criticism that is so central to both *Rudin* and *A Nest of Gentry*—and in the former novel it is criticism that marks Turgenev's own disdain for the language of philosophy, revelation, and abstraction.

Turgenev's disdain for "philosophizing" is matched by
his scorn for the lust for significance; in another letter to
his friend Evgeniya Lambert, Turgenev reproaches her for
her longing for perpetual "significance." The reproach is
articulated in terms that are essential to his own narrative:

> You're wrong to say it's better if we don't see one another
> frequently. . . . What does it matter if occasionally during
> these meetings, especially when others are there—the con-
> versation takes a light, frivolous turn. . . . As long as there's
> no vanity in your heart, for that's also a kind of pride. I re-
> member how as a young man I wanted every moment to be
> significant . . . an impertinent and far from innocent long-
> ing! Let the stream murmur to itself until it reaches the sea.
> (P, III, 386)

The longing for all of life to be "significant," with which
Turgenev here reprimands his pious friend, is a longing he
seems to have associated with youth. In *Fathers and Children* it is the youthful Arkady who longs for significance:
"One should structure life so that every moment is signif-

icant—Arkady murmured thoughtfully" (VIII, 324). At novel's end, this enthusiastic disciple of Turgenev's nihilist has become the character to whom is given the chance of continuity and "everyday happiness," the chance to perpetuate the life of his father, a life at peace with nature and himself. There seems little doubt that, for Turgenev, such life was "significant"—but it also seems clear that for the disciple Arkady significance meant something other than domestic life with Katya: it meant, perhaps, struggle and defiance, an articulation in word and gesture of the "principles" of nihilism. Despite the destructive implications of nihilism, Arkady seems to grasp it as a system, an ideology, that will endow his life with meaning. Bazarov is perhaps more consistent in scorning his friend's longings for "significance."

Rudin, Turgenev's first great hero of ideas, enters the salons of the provincial gentry with much the same aspirations as Arkady: to construe life as incessantly *significant*. In the character Rudin the youthful longing for significance is bound up with German metaphysics—whose Russian adherents were so adept at naming significance and so inept at simply living.[9] Bakunin boasted in a letter of 1836 to have lived not a single moment of life without consciousness.[10] Significance for the Idealists meant consciousness of the Idea, consciousness of oneself as the instrument of Being.[11] To claim life's significance as Rudin does is to claim that life *signifies* to the extent that it points to something beyond itself: "Rudin spoke of what gives eternal significance to the momentary life of man" (VI, 269). Rudin's eloquence is an attempt to render life as metaphor—to see its meaning in eternity, not in time; in poetry, not in prose. It is these attempts to jump out of causality—to escape consequence and temporality—that Turgenev's text finally condemns. It is a condemnation that has import for Turgenev's own understanding of "meaning" and the significant in life: meaning for Turgenev that is temporal, linear, "prosaic," meaning that is de-

Rudin's predilection for turning experience into language—an ability that entertains and charms in the Lasunskaya salon—is here judged as despotic; the reader is persuaded to agree when Rudin repeats his callousness in relations with Natalya and Volyntsev. Rudin's tyranny of analysis, of naming, is suggested again in Lezhnev's narrative of the Pokorsky circle: "Harmonious order was established in everything that we knew. . . . Nothing remained senseless or accidental . . . everything took on a clear, and at the same time mysterious, significance" (VI, 298).

The rhetorician's more intimate discourse is another species of analysis and dissection: Lasunskaya enjoys Rudin's talent at "definition," his ability to sum up character in a few words. "Voilà m-r Pigassof enterré [You've buried M. Pigassof]—what a master you are at defining a man" (VI, 273). She will later liken Rudin's talent to the work of a chiseler: "When you talk, vous gravez comme un burin" (VI, 275). Similar to Lezhnev's metaphor of the butterfly and the pin, Lasunskaya's analogy suggests chill analysis, the violation of a placid surface. Rudin's gossip—like his dialectic—aims at definitive statement, at finality: a strategy implicitly at odds with a narrative that leaves its central figure open to reevaluation, whose final summation is enigmatic.

The reproach to which Rudin is most open, and from which Lezhnev ultimately tries to save him, is of insincerity. Rudin himself seems conscious of this in conversation with Volyntsev: "I hope that you can no longer doubt my sincerity." Rudin's pleas for good faith draw the customarily silent Volyntsev into indignant response: "What seems sincere to you seems obtrusive and immodest to us" (VI, 316). Despite the reader's possible reluctance to grant Rudin sympathy, it seems that Turgenev's implication is that the fault is indeed more the words' than the man's: that it is the eloquence and rhetorical facility that has carried Rudin beyond responsibility, that he is himself to a certain degree a victim of language.

Turgenev's implication is that, once initiated, a stream of eloquence has its own momentum—for both speaker and listener; the insight is one he directed at himself as well. In a letter of 1853 to the literary critic Pavel Annenkov, Turgenev started to describe his delighted affection for Marya Nikolaevna Tolstaya, a sister of Leo Tolstoy, whom he had just met. He enumerates her virtues, and concludes: "I haven't encountered in a long time such grace, such touching charm. . . . I'll stop now so I won't start lying" (P, II, 240). This interruption of eloquence in midflow, this circumspection, is jestful but principled: Turgenev connects being "carried away," facility of speech, with lying. It is a vice with which he himself was reproached as a young man, and accounts for the radically divergent impressions of him recorded in memoirs. Turgenev was, apparently, incredibly adept at eloquent dissimulation.[17]

Rudin's eloquence combines the pretensions of German philosophy with the dubious sincerity of the man of the world: that Rudin initially charms both Basistov and Lasunskaya only affirms that he combines, for awhile, wit and wisdom (*um* in both its meanings).[18] Both forms of eloquence seem for Turgenev to represent sounds spun in a vacuum: what he offers as a challenge to eloquence are, paradoxically, various forms of silence—and speech that is elementally sincere.

Turgenev's novel of drawing rooms and eloquence opens with a room of a very different sort, and with language that is minimal in its unselfconsciousness. The novel's first scene takes Alexandra Lipina to the hovel of a dying peasant; the language of suffering is a language of sincerity drawn into the novel in its opening scene. It is, as it were, the minimal language against which later pretensions might be heard. It is also an articulation of that "voice of nature" that will subsequently be the object of Pigasov's salon wit. One of Pigasov's first anecdotes in chapter 2 describes his claim to have elicited from an artificial young lady the "voice of nature," a "true, unfeigned expression of feeling" (VI, 251). What Pigasov alludes to parodically, and what Turgenev renders dramatically, is the disparity between genuine expression and the artifice and feigning of society—terms that were central to eighteenth-century thinking about language.[19] What Turgenev's novel implicitly sketches is a spectrum of sincerity in language—where sincerity is grounded in silence and elemental gesture, and abandoned in forms of rhetoric that exist only for themselves, liberated from referentiality. Both Pigasov and Rudin—the first in his cynical disdain for common truth, the second in his pretensions to occult significance—abandon silence and beneficent gesture, which are for Turgenev the warrants of sincerity and truth. The reproach of untruth falls even on Lezhnev, whose final, eloquent praise of Rudin refers to the past, and not to the present. The novel's ending thus further complicates the relationship between sincerity and truth, for both Rudin and Lezhnev are caught in gestures of sincerity (a toast, a raised banner) whose truth is dubious. Turgenev's ending, with its ambiguous gesture—of heroism or defeat?—serves only to confirm what Lezhnev had earlier proclaimed: we never possess the "whole truth."

The characters who are finally granted happiness in Turgenev's novel are those who have the gift of silence—who, in the words of the narrator of "Journey into the Woodland," "know how to be silent [*umeiut molchat'*]." Turgenev's story ends with a benediction of men who even in their sufferings keep silent: "This one knows how not to complain" (VII, 70). Turgenev's implication in this tale is that the peasant's silence is the obverse of the narrator's own morbid, verbose regrets; it is a silence and measure that the man of wordy consciousness may envy.

Turgenev ends *Rudin* with weddings that join the novel's "silent ones": Lipina and Lezhnev, Natalya and Volyntsev. Lipina, in Lezhnev's words, is a woman in whose presence it is both easier to speak and to be silent: "With her you talk better, and it's easier to be silent" (VI, 318). Volyntsev is a good man, with no facility in speech. What these characters possess—as does the peasant guide of "Journey into the Woodland"—is a capacity for silence that Turgenev clearly admired, which fascinated him as evidence of unselfconsciousness, as a pledge of that immediacy and wholeness from which his Hamlets have been forever excluded. Professions of ineffability become a *topos* of Turgenev's prose; in *A Nest of Gentry* Turgenev's narrator refuses to name what occurs in the "pure soul of a young girl": "Words cannot express what took place in the girl's pure soul: it was a secret even to herself; let it remain a secret for everyone" (VII, 234). What is significant here is that Turgenev's narrators claim, and his "pure" characters demonstrate, the lack of precisely that facility that Rudin has: the facility of naming. Speech for Turgenev, especially speech about inner states and "ultimate" realities, is almost inevitably associated with brokenness, with the liabilities of lying. Turgenev's own indirection, and his preference for inarticulate characters, is his way of avoiding both deceit and the "poison" of consciousness.

Turgenev's most explicit essay in the articulation of consciousness is his "Diary of a Superfluous Man," a work that is his most "Dostoevskian" piece, and one that raises explicitly the problem of consciousness and language. Turgenev's narrator sets out to recount his life story, but falls into sentimental profusions and what he calls "speculation" (*umozrenie*—literally, a looking at the mind); the project of sincerity is confounded by his own convoluted rhetoric. "I pronounced words truly only in my youth; in my more mature years I've always managed to break myself in two" (V, 188). The superfluous man, like all of Turgenev's broken characters, is by definition incapable of speaking truthfully; Turgenev's unified, whole characters typically exist in a state that is either literally silent or minimally verbal. "Mumu," Turgenev's tale of a mute peasant and his capacity for love, creates in its hero, Gerasim, a figure of sentience without language; the work is emblematic of Turgenev's aesthetics as a whole, implying the conjunction of an artist's craft with silent experience.[20] The possibility that in speaking one will "break" (*perelomit'*) oneself always lurks in Turgenev's prose; we recall the anxiety of his letter about Tolstaya, that even well-intentioned eloquence becomes a form of lying.

The task confronting all narrative—and contemporary Russian literature—was, for Turgenev, the overcoming of romantic eloquence, a task he articulated as metaphoric murder. In a letter of 1857 to Pavel Annenkov, Turgenev spoke disdainfully of the Russian painter Bryullov, whose work was idolized by the Russian painters living in Italy, with whom Turgenev was acquainted: "By the way, I've had terrible rows here with Russian painters. Imagine, . . . they . . . senselessly babble one name: Bryullov, and without a moment's hesitation call all other painters idiots, beginning with Raphael." Such adulation was distressing to Turgenev because he regarded Bryullov as the incarnation of rhetoricism and falsehood in painting. What is interesting, and pertinent to Turgenev's own aesthetic, is his insistence that true art begins with the death of rhetoric: with the killing of Bryullov and Marlinsky—the latter being the author who epitomized, for Turgenev's generation, the excesses of Russian romantic rhetoric. "We will begin to have art only when Bryullov is killed, as Marlinsky was. . . . Bryullov—that phrase-monger without an ideal in his soul, that drum, that cold and clamorous rhetorician—has become the idol, the banner of our artists!" (P, III, 175). The terms with which Turgenev describes Bryullov—phrase-monger, drum, rhetorician—describe Turgenev's eloquent hero Rudin as well, whose stunning rhetoric captivates at first but is meant ultimately to be discarded for less epiphanic truths. Rhetoric must be killed, to be replaced by simpler speech—or silence. Turgenev's novel opens with a gesture of charity in the face of death; the hero's final deed is, I believe, an attempt to achieve the same simplicity and fullness as was imaged in Lipina's visit. Rudin himself abandons his own rhetoric; it is in Ru-

din's rueful regret, not in Lezhnev's peroration, that the
reader finally discovers compassion for this hero.

Rudin's taking to the barricades is intended as a gesture
of immediacy, a gesture that signifies not by reference to
some other world but by its solidarity, its presence in the
here and now. To call a gesture both simple and full—as I
have called Lipina's visit to a peasant hut, her offer of
medicine and tea—implies its unqualified goodness, its
lack of ambiguity. Rudin's final gesture is fraught with ambiguity, however: we cannot judge whether he falls as
hero or victim; he remains anonymous—or misnamed—to
his fellow soldiers. "—Tiens! said one of the retreating in-
surgents to the other,—on vient de tuer le Polonais. [Hold
on! . . . They've just killed the Pole.] . . . This 'Polonais'
was—Dmitry Rudin" (VI, 367). Such ambiguity seems
characteristic of all gesture in Turgenev, however—a gesture once performed, or spoken, becomes prey to misin-
terpretation. Even Lipina's charity is suspect: Lezhnev
asks her if she hasn't done it merely to please Lasunskaya—or if, conversely, she won't abandon "good
works" once her friend does.

No amount of knowledge can ever remove this essential
ambiguity of motive: Turgenev makes duality a necessary
aspect of the social—one that he ridicules and satirizes in
a character like Pandalevsky, but that is present even in
society's loftiest members: "By the way, reader, have you
noticed that a person who is extraordinarily absent-
minded among his subordinates is never absent-minded
with superiors? Now why is that? But such questions will
get us nowhere" (VI, 247). Natalya's experience in the
novel is an education in reading social behavior. It is, however, an experience that can only teach caution, can never
train her to avoid life's ambiguities. Sincerity, the novel
seems to say, cannot be a standard of judgment because it
can never be known: not just Rudin's but Lipina's, and
Lezhnev's, sincerity are obscure, perhaps even to themselves.

The novel's opening, with its seemingly unambiguous,

elemental dialogue of word and gesture, recalls in this sense Turgenev's longing for simplicity, for that unalloyed truth that his own novel qualifies. The setting of that opening scene assures us that we are in the presence of life's absolutes: pain and death. Such absolutes do not go far, however, in resolving the novel's complexities; they only render more acute the hero's longing to achieve—in the face of death—an act of truth.

The longing to kill rhetoric, the "clamorous rhetorician" is also, in its essence, a longing to dispense with language, to return to pure gesture, to clarity. To turn to Turgenev's own oppositions elsewhere, it is a longing to be done with Hamletic qualifications, to dramatize Quixotic simplicity. The longing on Turgenev's part to dispense with language is, as I suggest in the next chapter, allied to Turgenev's lyricism, and to his critique of social feigning and dissimulation. The longing is also associated with his revulsion at the labyrinths of consciousness, the paralyzing powers of the mind to spin rhetorical qualifications. There is a strong preference in Turgenev for the unselfconscious, the "as yet unspoken," the silent: hence his silent, strong women, from Natalya in *Rudin* to the heroine of his poem in prose, "The Threshold." In a characterization of the heroine Marianna in *Virgin Soil*—words that Leo Tolstoy would later recall—Turgenev reiterated what is a rule of all his art: only that is strong in us that remains a half-guessed mystery, even to ourselves (XII, 100).[21] What is characteristic of Turgenev—and what perhaps makes speaking of his work so difficult—is his representation of a state of wordlessness, a state for which the word-burdened artist longs. Turgenev's reluctance to trace with words the movements of consciousness, of motive and counter-motive, stem both from his sense of the ultimate unknowability of such motives, and from his longing to preserve a realm of purity, of "half-guessed mystery," of unconsciousness. One could amass endless examples of such representation; I will quote an example from *Fathers and Children*, which describes Katya's realization of Arkady's love for her: "Little by little a crimson blush spread lightly on her cheeks; her lips, though, didn't smile, and her dark eyes expressed disbelief and some other, as yet unnamed emotion" (VIII, 368).

The "as yet unnamed emotion" is very much the province of Turgenev's art. The tendency of modernity is to name the depths: Turgenev's characters, and his narratives, typically resist what seems a tyranny of naming. It is such tyranny that Bazarov rebuffs when Odintseva flirtatiously demands that he tell her "what is happening in him now": "What is happening!—Bazarov repeated—just as if I were some kind of government or society! In any case it's not at all interesting; and anyway, do you think a man can always say aloud everything that's happening in him?" (VIII, 298).

The "as yet unnamed emotion" is depicted—in its surface manifestations—but it is not named, for one cannot pronounce what is "happening" inside oneself, or within the other. These passages recall Turgenev's criticisms of Ostrovsky's drama, "The Poor Bride," and his insistence in his review that the "psychologist must disappear in the artist" (V, 391). Turgenev's rule of good dramaturgy is also a rule for his own narrative: "[Ostrovsky's] false manner consists in the extremely detailed and exhausting reproduction of all the bits and pieces of each personality, in a sort of false psychological analysis, which usually ends with each character endlessly repeating the same words, which the author feels express his uniqueness [*osobennost'*]" (V, 390). What Turgenev opposes to this aesthetics of self-statement, of the enunciation of self, is an aesthetics of gesture—of unconscious revelation: "Dearest of all to us are those simple, sudden movements in which the human soul audibly [*zvuchno*] expresses itself" (V, 392). Audible here are not words but gestures. These aesthetics of gesture, and of indirect revelation in everyday speech, will be Turgenev's own; that he articulates them in speaking of drama only suggests once more the connection of his novels to certain forms of dramatic expressiveness. Turgenev

will repeatedly resort to essentially dramatic strategies—
the showing of a character's facial changes when the company has left—with comic intent. In Rudin's final action,
however, gesture seems an attempt to express directly, immediately, all that the hero's eloquence has failed to convey or achieve. Turgenev puts his aesthetics of intimacy
here to a grander—political—use, recapitulates the intellectual's longing for signifying action.

What characterizes both *Rudin* and "Journey into the
Woodland" is an apparently self-conscious effort on the
author's part to move from the rhetoric of romanticism to
a discourse that is grounded in shared speech, in daily life.
Accompanying this rhetorical shift is a commitment to the
complexity of appearances—the enigmas and truths of the
everyday—rather than to an occult "beyond." Both these
works, I have suggested, are exemplary of Turgenev's poetics. Those poetics are not unambiguously realistic, nor
are they ever free of the legacy of poetry, of Idealism, of
lyrical despair. The overcoming that these works narrate is
belied by Turgenev's own prose—prose that bears the
marks of his poetic apprenticeship. Turgenev's tendency
to literary allusion, his elegant construction of verbal echoes and symmetries of structure, give to his novels a poetic density that asks that the reader "dig" for their meanings. Turgenev's own literary language is grounded in the
paradox of his own longings: the longings of a man of consciousness for the wordlessness of immediacy, the longings of a poet burdened with the legacies of literary tradition for the directness of peasant speech, the longing of
the intellectual for the silences of the everyday.

Chapter Two

GOSSIP, SILENCE, STORY:
LANGUAGE IN *A NEST OF GENTRY*

"I fear, I avoid phrases; but the fear of phrases is
also a pretension."
(XIII, 212)

THE GENTRY manors of Turgenev's novels are places so intimately known that in his rendering of them he discloses
far more than the living space of fictional characters. The
"nests" of his gentry are the dwelling places of his observations, his intuitions, his thoughts—and in their very description those thoughts and intuitions are made material
and apparent. Turgenev's manors, the paths to and from
the gentry nests, their corners and drawing rooms—all
provide exceptionally fortuitous examples of how Turgenev's prose "thinks" concretely.[1]

In *A Nest of Gentry* the architecture of the Kalitin household describes a world that is morally fractured—a single
dwelling that contains two opposed realms. The topography of these two worlds is clearly delineated: the primary,
visible world is Marya's; her kingdom is the drawing
room. The hidden, removed world is Marfa's, her upper
room a "family state" [*semeinyi shtat*] that stands in opposition to Marya's "society" [*svet*] below. The two worlds
are carefully developed and juxtaposed by Turgenev; he
uses them to suggest a double vision of the plot that will
unfold. The hero Lavretsky passes through both worlds,
through both drawing room and upper room, in his home-
ward journey. The drawing room and upper room likewise provide different "readings" of him and of his fate;

they cast his story as either tragedy or melodrama. If Turgenev's narrative household is his stage—and the dramatic background of his prose is always evident[2]—it is a stage where the same audience can watch two productions. His houses are commodious and subtle.

The realms of Turgenev's novel are distinguished, however, not only in architectural terms, but in linguistic terms as well. Turgenev's second novel is concerned with the way people speak—about faith, about behavior, about forgiveness and love—and *A Nest of Gentry* sustains a careful and complex juxtaposition of hypocritical and true speaking. The architectural oppositions of the novel are complemented by linguistic ones: the language of Marya's drawing room is opposed to that of Marfa's hidden room. Turgenev's novel is satirical of gentry piety and moral sententiousness, but it is something else as well, effecting a movement beyond satire in its implication of a realm of positive communication. The lower stage of *A Nest of Gentry*—a world of hypocrisy and gossip, a world whose plots derive from society tales and the theater of melodrama, is countered by a higher, tragic stage. The implications of this countering are, for Turgenev, both historical and aesthetic, formulating hopes for Russia's future, and defending the contemplative's place in society.

Turgenev articulated the special tensions of life in metaphors of language and space in one of his *Poems in Prose*, written toward the end of his literary career. Turgenev puts it thus in "The Phrase" of 1871:

> I fear, I avoid phrases; but the fear of phrases is also a pretension.
>
> Thus, between these two foreign words, between pretension and phrases, our complex life rumbles and hesitates.
> (XIII, 212)

This sensitivity to the way language shapes both world and the self, the way language limits the imaginations of being and becoming, is a concern that can be traced throughout Turgenev's artistic career. Its genesis lies, without doubt, in his Idealistic apprenticeship in Germany and in the Russian circles of the 1840s. The inflated ambitions of Hegelian rhetoricians, and their distance from human experience, left in Turgenev's work a residue of skepticism toward their linguistic presumptions, and a generally heightened sensitivity to the resonances and implications of "ordinary" conversation.[3]

The much older Turgenev of the *Poems in Prose* is an artist still acutely attentive to language, as conscious of its limits and illusions, as of its transfiguring possibilities. Language as such constitutes the theme of no less than five of these prose pieces: in "The Phrase," the artist proclaims the conundrum of speech, truth, and artifice; in "The Chalice," he compares his art to the work of a master goldsmith, whose craft both comforts and kills; in "The Russian Language" he claims his native tongue as pledge of freedom and dignity; and finally, in "Prayer," which immediately precedes "The Russian Language" in Turgenev's final sequence, the writer meditates on the speech of prayer, on dialogue and truth.

The meditation on language that is sustained throughout these two cycles of prose poems is not an isolated event in Turgenev's oeuvre; the poems are, in fact, recapitulations of earlier concerns, returns to problems addressed much earlier, in other literary forms. Turgenev's first novelistic hero, Rudin, stands both as culminating figure in the author's line of verbal deceivers, and as his fullest, most complex examination of the powers and perils of speech.

Turgenev opened his career as a prose writer with a series of studies of Russian Hamlets—studies that examine both the ethical and ontological consequences of their attitudes toward language. Turgenev's superfluous man, Chulkaturin (who is, perhaps, as much a figure for the always-observing artist, as for the alienated gentry intellectual) pronounces in his *Diary* a paradox that much of Turgenev's prose was to explore: "Between my feelings and thoughts—and the expression of these feelings and thoughts—there lay some senseless, incomprehensible and insurmountable obstacle" (V, 186). The disjunction of language and being is the disquieting given that underlies all of Turgenev's efforts to narrate life. The attempt to reconstitute wholeness and purity of speech is the implicit aim of all of his writing; it is the ideal which governs his antipathy to the verbal psychologizing of Tolstoy and Dostoevsky.[4]

Turgenev's prose poems on language recall the topics of his novels and novellas: the artist thinking about the implications of his craft was also the author of the "social" novels. That we find meta-literary allusions in Turgenev's novels does not deny their historicity, or their concern with Russian society; it does, however, qualify our understanding of their realism, and forces us to rethink connections between the aesthetic and the historical in his work. The Russian language, Turgenev declares in the eponymous poem, is "truthful and free" (*pravdivyi i svobodnyi*) (XII, 199). This, however, is a statement of potential, of a state (linguistic but also political) where truth and freedom reign. That state, in Turgenev's day as in our own, is unattained—and the object of Turgenev's attention is characteristically not the realm of this pure and potential speech but the realm of "The Phrase"—where complex life jostles between pretense and phrases.

The terms that Turgenev so explicitly states in these elder meditations place the linguistic poles of his narrative worlds: the implicit realm of speech that is true and free; the fallen world necessarily caught between varieties of artificial speaking; the dialogic rejection of unequivocal truth; the consciousness of craftsmanship, of art as verbal consolation. Turgenev's prose poems give us in epigrammatic and elliptic form what has been present all along: the concerns of an artist for whom the spectacle of human life always alluded to problematic creativity, whose "stories" are never innocent or transparent. These prose poems are purified of narratives that they nonetheless recall—not as commentary but as complement, so that the "late" Turgenev evokes the younger artist. I use these short pieces not as mere glosses to *A Nest of Gentry* or to other of Turgenev's narrative works, but as prologue, as meditations that make us conscious of concerns voiced less lyrically in the novel itself.

The specificity of *A Nest of Gentry* lies in its attention to language as a function of place—as its title proclaims, the novel is about a particular space in the world, a "gentry nest." The moral concerns of the novel emerge as a counterpoint of places in which people speak—hypocritically or truly. The world and words come together in the novel in a crucial joining of the philosophical and historical. The architectural construction of spiritual hierarchy in *A Nest of Gentry* (where Marfa's room lies, both literally and figuratively, above the salon of Marya) supports the plotting of truth and deceit in the novel's world: the feigning of Marya's lower realm is implicitly opposed to the authenticity of Marfa's room. The repetitions and echoings of language in Turgenev's novel explore language in its sameness and difference, spoken in being and in dissembling. The theatrical metaphors of the novel's lower realm develop Turgenev's opposition of spectral and true existence, casting his lesser characters as speakers of scripts that are not their own.

The eminent formalist critic Boris Eikhenbaum, writing of Tolstoy, noted provocatively—if briefly—that Turgenev's novels are essentially "society tales" updated.[5] Eikhenbaum here likens Turgenev's novels to a genre of the 1830s in Russia, to narratives of romance and intrigue in high society, characterized by gossip, hypocrisy, and the victimization of innocence.[6] Salon banter is clearly a crucial element of Turgenev's novels, particularly in *A Nest of Gentry*. What Eikhenbaum's comment fails to take account of, however, is the other linguistic pole of Turgenev's novels, a pole represented in *A Nest of Gentry* by the monastery and by the "river depth" of Lavretsky's country estate at Vasilevskoe—both places identified with contemplative silence and submergence in Being. Turgenev's dialogue, even in its most witty and satirical moments, is held by a lyric, contemplative frame that moves toward silence. The meaning that is emptied from language in salon discourse is returned to it in movement away from "the world." The moments of silence within Turgenev's text, and the natural and holy silence that frame his "social" novel, are intended as returns to a being that has been lost in the fallen babel of "the world." The echoings and juxtapositions of Turgenev's texts are all part of this renewal, his shuttling (as he put it) between phrases and pretentiousness in a quest for "complex life" and truth.

Turgenev's novel attempts to return to language some of the meaning that is lost in merely social discourse. His novel is grounded in salon dialogue, but it also draws on lyric, and on the silence, the unspokenness, which is figurally placed within the novel in Marfa's room and at Vasilevskoe. Silence is itself something that Turgenev wrote of repeatedly—in letters and in narratives, as an aesthetic ideal and as an attribute of character. Silence is, for Turgenev, variously Tyutchevan and Pascalian, lyric and philosophical, naive and tragic. It is a crucial aspect of his own aesthetic restraint, and one to which I shall return in the conclusion of this essay.

Turgenev's second novel unfolds as a perfectly symmetrical series of narrative movements that carry the hero Lavretsky to Vasilevskoe and hope—and then out again. In the first movement, chapters 1–7, Turgenev presents the Kalitin household and the arrival of Lavretsky. The novel's double moral vision is presented, and the movement ends with a brief coda that renders a final juxtaposition of Marya's and Marfa's worlds. In the novel's second movement, that narrative leaps back in time, to present Lavretsky's genealogy—a genealogy that brings him finally to marriage with Varvara, Paris, and adulterous deceptions. The third movement returns with Lavretsky to Russia, and after a brief reprise of the "two worlds" at the Kalitin household, the hero journeys deeper into the countryside, to his estate. This central movement of the novel constitutes Lav-retsky's encounter with the cradle of his childhood, with his homeland (*rodina*), and with Liza: encounters that together symbolize the implicit fullness of his quest. This movement ends (chapters 34 and 35) with Lavretsky and Liza embracing in the garden, and with the brief biography of Liza. The return of Varvara initiates the novel's fourth movement (chapters 36–45) that closes with the retreat of both Liza and Lavretsky from a scene now dominated by Varvara. In the epilogue, Turgenev sketches a final movement that suggests another, idyllic stage in which the fate of characters might be pastoral, and not tragic.

Turgenev begins his novel with a description of two women sitting before an open window—"framing" them quite literally, as he will repeatedly frame his characters throughout the text. This particular visual device, however, frames both the female figures and Turgenev's narrative: the window through which we enter their lives also establishes firmly one of the novel's implicit boundaries. The broad, clear sky of the first sentence, the azure depth (*glub' lazuri*), is abandoned for a more intimate setting— but the open expanse stands always as a kind of background to the narrative, the novel's "Beyond." It is the same beyond alluded to in the novel's final paragraph— ineffable and hidden. Of Liza and Lavretsky the narrator says, "What were they thinking? What were they feeling? Who can know? Who can say? There are certain moments, certain feelings in life. . . . One can only point to them— and walk by" (VII, 294). At the end of his novel Turgenev will return us to this realm of what cannot be spoken— what escapes speech. The novel itself, however, exists in another realm, the realm of conversation, gossip, argument, confrontation, flattery. Nonetheless, Turgenev's narrative seeks, paradoxically, precisely that realm of what is unspoken, seeks it within a world of compromised speech. In moving from beginning to end, from vision of sky to silence, one of the things the novel looks for is true speech. It looks for such speech inside the manor—

through the window, in the world inhabited by Marya and Marfa.

These two women are visually juxtaposed in the novel's opening description; the narrator goes on—in the first and subsequent chapters—to develop the two as opposing moral voices. In the novel's world, Marya is the voice of hypocrisy, and Marfa the voice of truth. Marya, the narrator tells us, is more sentimental than good; Marfa is independent, and always speaks her mind (VII, 126). In their first conversation, Marya sighs and pines, while Marfa, who is knitting, complains about Marya's companion and gossip, Gedeonovsky. Characteristically, Turgenev is concerned, in this first scene, to establish the relative trustworthiness of his speakers, and also to raise the issue of truth in speech per se. The author of *Rudin* shows himself as sensitive as ever to the nuance of deceit.

In the women's first exchange, Marfa seems to demand of Marya a literalness of expression with which the younger woman is unconcerned:

What's that about?—[Marfa] suddenly asked Marya Dmitrievna—What are you sighing about, my dear?
Just so—she said—what wonderful clouds!
What, are you sorry for them? (VII, 128)

From this somewhat humorous statement of incongruity Marfa moves on to discuss Gedeonovsky who, according to her, is little better than a liar. Lying and gossip are, in fact, inseparable for Marfa: "He looks like such a meek one . . . and as soon as he opens his mouth he either tells a lie or starts to gossip." And when Marya tries to excuse him—his education is poor, he doesn't speak French—Marfa again insists: "It would be better if he didn't speak any language: he wouldn't lie" (VII, 128).

This association of gossip, lying, and Marya's sentimentality—implicitly contrasted with Marfa's outspokenness—is continued in chapter 2. With the arrival of Gedeonovsky, and his news of Lavretsky's return to Russia, conversation turns to his marriage and its demise. This exchange on Lavretsky and marriage becomes an exemplary collision of the novel's two moral views. The opposition of sentimental gossip and blunt truth-saying in chapter 1 is carried further here, and given a topic: Lavretsky's marriage and his responsibility for what happened. Marya and Gedeonovsky judge Lavretsky harshly—implying that he should be ashamed to appear in society. Marfa, outraged, objects—and ridicules the blatant hypocrisy of their position.

> . . . what kind of nonsense is that? The man's come back to his homeland—Where would you have him go? And he was hardly to blame!
> —The husband is always guilty . . . when his wife behaves badly.
> —You say that, my dear, because you yourself haven't been married. (VII, 129)

Marfa goes on to say that Lavretsky's guilt lay only in spoiling his wife—and expresses her general doubt of the wisdom of love matches. At this point Marfa leaves—and Marya and Gedeonovsky proceed to do just what Marfa had predicted they would: they gossip about her. Their conversation, in fact, returns to the problem of dissemblance, what Marfa had lumped together as "gossip, dissemblance, and fabrication": the scarf she is knitting, she told Gedeonovsky, "is intended for someone who never gossips, isn't crafty and doesn't invent stories, if only there exists such a person in the world" (VII, 130). Gedeonovsky's defense is the standard lame appeal: "That's how times are [vek uzh takoi]"—everyone dissembles (even chickens, in his anecdote)—then how (or why) am I not to? Gedeonovsky's is an easy dismissal of Marfa, and is quickly succeeded by their primary topic: Lavretsky. The balance of the conversation between Marya and Gedeonovsky is classic Turgenev satire: conspiratorial whispers, delight at Lavretsky's misfortune, obvious relishing of the very publicness of the scandal they claim to deplore. Gedeonovsky's final attempt at "morality"—on the subject of women's behavior—is interspersed (and thus rendered ri-diculous) with the narrator's description of his daubing his eyes with a handkerchief (VII, 131).

Turgenev's satire of the gentry here has to do with their moral hypocrisy—a hypocrisy of speech that pretends to touch on moral questions of the most serious nature. The issue that Marya and Gedeonovsky make into a matter for racy speculation is, after all, Lavretsky's life tragedy. Their discussion of his marriage and his fate, however, devalues it; Marfa's equation of gossip and lying suggests that the salon narration of Lavretsky's story lies about it, in a par-ticularly dangerous way. The discourse of Marya's draw-ing room is, implicitly, the discourse of Russia's elite: that discourse has pretensions to be the ethical voice of society. Marfa's clear, honest voice does not belong to the drawing room: her blunt speech and moral vision are exceptions there; she lives, both literally and figuratively, elsewhere. Marfa's independence from the drawing room is a source of strength—but also a concession of realms. It is Marya who reigns in the lower room; her sentimentality and gos-sip are its language of morality and feeling.

What happens in Marya's realm is that private life is turned into public discourse and gossip. This conversion of the private into public currency—both narrative and monetary—is implicit in another of the novel's stories, that of Lavretsky's romance with Varvara, and her entry into the Parisian social whirl. Varvara's infidelity—her betrayal of the marriage vow—figures in the novel as a betrayal of another sort, as well. Her surrender of intimate life to the gossip columns of Paris constitutes a prostitution of self that, in *A Nest of Gentry*, stands at opposite poles from Li-za's virginity and silence.

Lavretsky falls in love with Varvara at the theater, and it is the relationship with her that will usher his life into the realm of the "spectacular" and thrust his life onto the cen-ter stage of European gossip. The theatrical meeting ground is significant because Varvara, like the dilletant Panshin, who is her true match, is a wholly public person, whose life is shaped as a consummately played role. Mikhalevich, the friend who introduces Lavretsky to Varvara, unconsciously states the truth of the matter when he calls Varvara "an amazing, brilliant creature, a performer [*artistka*] in the real sense of the word" (VII, 167). The theatrical metaphors, and the watching of his beloved as she watches the play, also recall Dumas—whose hero first sees, and meets, *la dame aux camélias* at a Parisian theater. Varvara is a character deserving of Dumas—an author Turgenev disliked[7]—and she enters fully into her role when she returns to Lavretsky in chapter 43 (in the epilogue, the narrator tells us that Varvara has found her human ideal—in the dramatic works of Dumas fils; VII, 288). Varvara, like Panshin and Marya, lives a life modeled on melodrama and racy romance; she is a character from the lower, nontragic, stage.

What Turgenev traces, in Varvara and in Lavretsky's infatuation with her, is the conversion of private life into public event, a conversion that Varvara encourages and on which she thrives. The summit of her accomplishment is Europe's knowledge of her. (The implication of biblical knowledge is active in Turgenev's text—what begins as gossip ends in adultery.) The publication of her life—making it printed, readable—confers reality on Varvara. The reality of the stage, of role playing, of gossip and gossip columns, is the only reality about which she knows or cares.

The "true artist" with whom Lavretsky falls in love is the daughter of parents ruined, it is hinted, by her father's shady dealings with Treasury funds. The dealings become an "event" (*istoriia*: a word that simultaneously denotes an occurrence and its transformation into public speech or "story"). The father's career is ruined (unlike his daughter's, whose "career" is furthered by *scandale*). "What came out was more than unpleasant, it was a sordid story. The general more or less extricated himself from the situation, but his career was finished" (VII, 168). The family moves to Moscow, delighted at their daughter's successful match. After a brief period on Lavretsky's estate, the couple moves to Paris, where Varvara proceeds to construct a brilliant reputation as mistress of a salon. She plays perfectly the role of Parisienne: "A week hadn't passed before she made her way across the street, wore a shawl, opened her umbrella and put on gloves no worse than the most pure-blooded Parisian woman" (VII, 173). Varvara's success is measured by her fame (*izvestnost'*): "*La belle madame de Lavretskii* soon became famous from the *chaussée d'Antin* to the *rue de Lille*" (VII, 173). The height of her achievement, however, comes when she begins to receive at her salon a certain "m-r Jules," a gossip columnist who is "offensive" to her but essential. He ensures her reputation by converting her life into public melodrama, read about day-in and day-out by the Parisian populace.

> This *m-r Jules* was quite offensive to Varvara Pavlovna, but she received him because he wrote for various papers and constantly referred to her . . . he told the entire world, i.e. several hundred subscribers, who had absolutely nothing to do with *m-me de l . . . tski*, how this lady, a true frenchwoman in wit (*une vraie française par l'esprit*) . . . was kind and amiable . . . in a word, he put out the word about her [*puskal o nei molvu po miru*]—and no matter what you say, that's pleasant. (VII, 173–174)[8]

Varvara has traded privacy for publicity. M. Jules makes her public, places her in the public domain—his column effects verbally what her affair with Ernest effects physically: her becoming public is a kind of prostitution, a desecration of intimacy, an allowing of all the world to enter one's private life. There is nothing hidden in Varvara's life, and her very reality seems to depend on its "fictionalization." She makes the blithe transaction as do all members of "le monde": she trades privacy for social (and fictional) reality.

In his description of Varvara's life and her betrayal of Lavretsky, Turgenev dwells with particular care on the conversion of their privacy into "news." The truth of Lavretsky's life comes back to him, alien, in the form of others' words. When he discovers the note from his wife's lover, Ernest, to "Betsy" (Varvara has, for Ernest, a different name, a different identity), he sees himself cast as the "old husband, terrible husband [*staryi muzh, groznyi muzh*]" of Pushkin's narrative poem, *The Gypsies*. The final linguistic conversion of Varvara's life occurs after Lavretsky has left her. He no longer has direct contact with his wife; he himself learns of her only through gossip columns: "Then increasingly bad rumors started to circulate; finally all the journals made much of a tragicomic story in which his wife played an unenviable role. It was all over: Varvara Pavlovna had become *an item* [*izvestnost'iu*]" (VII, 178).

This passage shows the coming to completion of a process set in motion at the theater: in surrendering himself to Varvara, Lavretsky has also surrendered himself to a world of roles and delusion, a world whose most appropriate expression is in the melodrama and gossip column. These are the artistic and verbal forms that express the only truths that world cares about; human experience is mere grist for a sentimental gossip mill.

To the fallen worlds of Paris and Marya's salon Turgenev opposes a series of narrative spaces that preserve true feeling and true speech—and a language of emotion that is, significantly, silent. The visual opposition of the novel's upper and lower realms, of hypocrisy and silence, is first sketched in chapter 7, in the brief passage that is a coda to the novel's first movement.

Lavretsky has arrived at the Kalitin household; he has spent an evening in Marya's drawing room. After this first evening, the company separate, and the narrator describes, in a passage separated by ellipses from the main body of the chapter, two scenes that occur simultaneously within the manorhouse. Turgenev makes central here the opposition of realms—upstairs and down—and the problem of authentic speech.

On that same day, at eleven o'clock in the evening, this is what was happening in Mrs. Kalitina's house. Downstairs, in the doorway of the drawing room, having seized an opportune moment, Vladimir Nikolaevich was saying goodbye to Liza, and as he held her hand he said to her: "You know who draws me here; you know why I am constantly coming to your house; what good are words, when all is clear anyway." Liza said nothing to him in reply, and without smiling, raising her eyebrows slightly and blushing, looked at the floor, but she didn't take away her hand; while upstairs, in Marfa Timofeevna's room, in the light of an icon lamp that hung before dim, ancient icons, Lavretsky sat in an armchair, his elbows on his knees and his face in his hands; the old woman, standing in front of him, now and then silently stroked his hair. He spent more than an hour with her, having already said goodbye to the lady of the house; he said almost nothing to his old, kind friend, and she asked nothing of him. . . . And what was there to say, what was there to ask about? She understood everything anyway, she already felt sympathy for everything that filled his heart to overflowing. (VII, 148)

What Turgenev has done, in this brief passage, is to juxtapose two scenes, which take place simultaneously, and that echo each other. The qualities of Turgenev's moral vision that link him to drama are particularly apparent here—as his domestic stage is split, and boldly displays its allegorical intent. "Downstairs," in the drawing room, Panshin tells Liza that there is no need for speaking between them, that all is clear; "upstairs," in Marfa's room, before her icons, there is real silence; it is the narrator who tells us that absolute understanding exists. Both realms use the same language; in the moral landscape of the novel, however, the lower realm is a world of compromised, deceptive speech. In the upper room statement is replaced by silence, deceit by mutuality. The narrator points to a state of spiritual congruence that cannot be spoken.

The silence that Turgenev depicts in his novel, and that represents the linguistic pole opposed to salon deceit and gossip, is crucially present in three different places in *A Nest of Gentry*: at Vasilevskoe, in Marfa's room, and finally in the monastery of Liza's ending. In these places Turgenev demonstrates moments of perceptive intuition impossible in Marya's lower realm; the silences of these places punctuate the narration of the lower world.

On returning to his estate, Lavretsky spends one day sitting outside, locked in "peaceful enthrallment" (*mirnoe otsepenenie*) (VII, 189). Lavretsky, the narrator tells us, is surrounded by quiet: his day of enthrallment is a day of contemplation, a day of silent submergence in an equally silent natural world:

> He sat under the window, motionless, and it was as though he was listening to the stream of quiet life that encircled him. . . . Once again he begins to listen to the quiet, expecting nothing—and at the same time as though constantly expecting something; quiet embraces him from all sides. (VII, 189–190)

Turgenev is describing here the inner state of a contemplative, absolutely still and silent, in whom volition is almost absent, replaced by a different kind of expectation. Lavretsky "descends" in this passage to a state in which the boundaries between self and nature are diminished, fluid—it is precisely fluidity that characterizes the imagery of Turgenev's description: Lavretsky himself is conscious of being on the "river bottom" (*na dne reki*). In this state of fluid silence, without will, Lavretsky is able to perceive what is imperceptible from any other vantage: he is struck by the quiet, the absence of hurry in this world, qualities of being he longs to embrace—or, rather, to which he longs to surrender. What he wishes to learn is the measure of the boredom (*skuka*) of the place: "Let it bring me peace, and prepare me to know how to act without haste" (VII, 190).

To learn to act without haste, to derive strength and

health from this "inert silence" (*bezdeistvennaia tish'*)—these are the longings of the contemplative Lavretsky. And he *is*, in this passage, a "contemplative." If Liza, in her final monastic enclosure, is the novel's orthodox contemplative, Lavretsky is the novel's contemplative of nature—a contemplative whose vision can be narrated (Liza's cannot), who perceives in nature a source of regeneration for both spirit and body. Liza's silence, like the object of her contemplation, occurs beyond the boundaries of narrative: Lavretsky's contemplation lies squarely at its center; the lyrical, silent center that holds the narrative.

Turgenev's narrative is rooted in this passage—both in the sense that this passage narrates the hero's rebirth, and in the sense that it alludes to the genesis of Turgenev's own vision, his own poetics. The moments of Lavretsky's contemplation—here and in the novel's epilogue—are the moments in which Turgenev draws closest to his hero, in which Turgenev most nearly depicts Lavretsky as a poet. Turgenev gives him, in these passages, the sensibilities and vision from which the novel is written. That is to say, Turgenev's own creative genius derives from this contemplative seeing, but beyond that, the capacity for such vision defines his human ideal. To be able to see simply is, in a sense, to have been returned to wholeness. Lavretsky does this—not perfectly, not in the duration of time—but for a moment.

Lavretsky's vision from this day of contemplation is almost more than vision, it is trans-sensual, involving his hearing and viscera as well as his sight. At the end of the chapter, Lavretsky looks skyward and sees sun and clouds: "The quiet embraces him from all sides, the sun moves through the calm blue sky, and the clouds swim quietly in it; it seems that they know where and why they are swimming. At the same time, in other places on earth, life was seething, rushing, rumbling" (VII, 190). Elsewhere in the world there is bustle and noise: here there is silence, vision, measure. Turgenev marks here Lavretsky's distance from that world of bustle and noise, the world he has left; Turgenev is also reminding us of the spiritual landscape of his novel, of Paris and the salon. What Lavretsky has left behind is the gossip, the deceit, the false speaking of Varvara and Marya; what he has come to is a silence, both inner and outer.

Turgenev describes the natural world here as silent—but the quality in this instance is positive, regenerative. In the novel that followed *A Nest of Gentry*, *On the Eve*, Turgenev's romantic artist Bersenev is alarmed at the notion of nature's silence: he longs still to hear Oberon's trumpet (VIII, 13). And in another of Turgenev's shorter narratives, "Journey into the Woodland," the spectacle of nature's silence gives cause for fear and trembling, it serves as reproach to human insignificance; Turgenev opens the piece with a clear reminiscence of Pascalian silence.[9] The human journey in this tale is, however, a journey toward vision— a vision akin to Lavretsky's at the center of *A Nest of Gentry*—in which the narrator's ability to contemplate an emerald fly constitutes the reward of his spiritual regeneration.[10] Turgenev's implication—in both "Journey into the Woodland" and *A Nest of Gentry*—is that this capacity for perception must be both way and goal. Silent contemplation in "Journey" stands opposed to romantic self-absorption and rhetorical effusion; in *A Nest of Gentry* it stands opposed to salon deceits, to a world of discourse that is groundless—powerful but ultimately ephemeral.

Turgenev places Lavretsky's contemplation quite intentionally: we are meant, I believe, to read this passage as central—both in his life and in the novel's movement. That Lavretsky's idyll is ultimately aborted does not diminish the importance of this center, which in fact holds the narrative.

There are important echoes of Lavretsky's vision in the novel's opening and ending, those passages that point "beyond" the human toward nature and the divine. The silence of true measure that is natural at the novel's center becomes domestic in Marfa's upper room. In *A Nest of Gen-*

try, Turgenev gives us silence of three kinds: natural, religious, and domestic. Each one of these is a reproach to the more visible, noisier life of a world for which silence—and the capacity to see—are alien.

The silence of the novel's ending is the silence of monasticism and prayer. Here again, silence is connected with rebirth, although for Liza, unlike Lavretsky, "rebirth" occurs as a symbolic rite of the church. Liza's spiritual silence is a kind of final realization of her wordlessness: Liza, who had "no words of her own," has devoted her life to The Word, to Being which transcends all speech. When Liza declares to Lavretsky that she has no words of her own, he thinks to himself: "Thank God." There is clear authorial intent—and perhaps irony—in the remark: it *is* thanks to God that Liza is wordless. The girl's statements about death and faith are not personal, they are the words of religious tradition; but there is yet another sense in which Liza is wordless. As the narrator tells us in his biography of the girl, "she had no 'words of her own,' but she had her own thoughts, and she went her own way" (VII, 243). The implication that one may have thoughts without words may appear alien to modern sensibilities, but the unnameability of God, the existence of Being beyond all naming, is in fact central to the Eastern Christian tradition.[11] Even if we dispense with this theological reading, Turgenev clearly intends to distinguish Liza radically from the characters of the novel who are made *only* of words: from Panshin, from Varvara, from the whole babbling company of Marya's salon. Turgenev upholds this notion of thoughts that exist free of words, although not in any divine sense. The silent demonstrations of forgiveness and compassion in Marfa's room are evidence of ineffability, the same silence with which the novel ends.

The final paragraph of Turgenev's novel is a refusal to speak: "the end," says the narrator, cannot be told, because Liza and Lavretsky have left the world: "What can one say about people still alive who have already left the world [*zemnoe poprishche*]" (VII, 293). "Plot" for Liza and

Lavretsky has ended: all that is left are moments—"moments in life, certain feelings . . . one can only point to them—and walk by." If we consider that Turgenev's novel has been a narration not merely of plot but of "moments," this disclaimer may seem disingenuous; but Turgenev in fact accomplishes here an apotheosis of what he disclaims. Turgenev's novel ends with a demonstration and defense of ineffability. In the body of his novel Turgenev showed us wordless moments in Marfa's "state": his ending proclaims the eternal unfathomability of the slightest gestures, life's evasion of all naming.

When Turgenev narrates the meetings of Lavretsky and Marfa, and later of Marfa and Liza, in the old woman's upper room, Turgenev gives us examples of unspoken communion that stand in radical opposition to the dissembling below. Like the novel's final paragraph, these passages are exclusively visual, as though, in a world of dissembling speech, we must learn merely to see and dispense with speaking. Marfa herself is gifted with an uncanny ability to see beneath the surface; the words she speaks—both her denunciations of Gedeonovsky and Panshin, and her allusive warnings to Lavretsky in chapter 42—come straight from her intuitive discernment (*prozorlivost'*). What goes unspoken in this exchange is the chance that Lavretsky might elope with Liza: "Give me your word of honor, that you're an honorable man.—If you will. But what for?—I know what for" (VII, 274).

If Vasilevskoe and the monastery represent, in the novel, poles of purity, Marfa's room is a kind of mediating realm, a world that partakes of silence and truth but remains within the gentry nest. The silence of nature and of God, which are the novel's farthest poles from salon discourse, stand nonetheless outside human community. In contrast, Marfa's "family state" remains within society, posits in fact a kind of utopian family that establishes its own kinships and language. That world mediates between a fallen society and holiness: Marfa descends to the salon to speak her mind; she also provides refuge upstairs for orphans, canaries, and cuckolded husbands. Liza's holiness is beyond the world, an icon of purity and stillness that exists in problematic relationship with the hypocrisy of the salon: Marfa's holiness is within the gentry nest, and Turgenev's design, it seems to me, suggests that the regeneration of Russia will come from this immanent holiness, and not from Liza's.

The idyllic social vision of the epilogue in fact derives from Marfa's community. In his ending, Turgenev describes a new world within old walls, a world of children, animals, and innocence. The children who are Russia's future have transferred unconventional kinships from the upper room to the salon. They have also banished hypocrisy with games and laughter. The laughter of children, in this vision, will purify and regenerate social discourse—a clearly utopian longing, darkened by reference to Gedeonovsky and the musician Lemm: the former still lies (*lzhet po-prezhnemu*), the latter's music is lost (*muzyki posle nego ne ostalos'?—Ne znaiu; edva li*) (VII, 291). The comic idyll is qualified by the residue of deceit and the evanescence of art.

When Varvara returns to Lavretsky, Turgenev returns to the novel's oppositions of theatricality and silence, in a farcical scene of false penitence that is juxtaposed with another of the novel's silent friezes. Again, Turgenev's technique is to create a counterpoint of public and private moments, of dialogue and narration, in which silence exposes hypocrisy. The "resurrected" Varvara enacts a lengthy confession and supplication: her appeal to Lavretsky is couched in religious terms (VII, 245). When Varvara goes to Marya Dmitrievna's, she repeats this sentimental litany of repentance: she speaks of duty, forgiveness, of her own deep "Russianness" (VII, 254–255). The scenes are ones of confession (by Varvara) and forgiveness (by Marya Dmitrievna). The women appropriate the language of religion and love of one's homeland, desecrating through hypocrisy the novel's implicit values. Turgenev inserts two significant elements of silence into this drawing room farce: Liza enters the drawing room while Varvara is there, and works silently at her needlework in the presence of the woman who has destroyed her hopes (VII, 258); the chapter closes with another upper room frieze, juxtaposed with the banter and gaming below: "Meanwhile, downstairs in the drawing room, they were playing preference" (VII, 261).

This chapter ends with a moment of true forgiveness, a moment juxtaposed with the false speech, the parodic forgiveness, of the salon:

> Liza went into her aunt's room and sank into the chair in utter exhaustion. Marfa Timofeevna looked at her for a long time in silence, quietly fell to her knees in front of her—and began, still in silence, to kiss each of her hands in turn. Liza moved forward, blushed—and started to cry, but she didn't lift Marfa Timofeevna up, and didn't take her hands away: she felt that she had no right to take them away, that she had no right to keep the old woman from expressing her repentance, her concern, from begging her forgiveness for yesterday: and Marfa Timofeevna couldn't stop kissing these poor, pale, helpless hands—and wordless tears poured from her eyes and from those of Liza; and Matros the cat meowed in the armchair beside a ball of wool and stocking, as the lengthening flame of the icon lamp barely moved and stirred before the icon; in the neighboring room, behind the door, stood Nastasya Karpovna and also dabbed her eyes in secret with a checked handkerchief wound into a tight little ball. (VII, 261)

The narrative "point" is that what Varvara professes (repentance, sorrow, humility, mutuality) is emptied of meaning below, but replenished with significance in its enactment above. Turgenev's description is a demonstration: *this* is what loving forgiveness is. His prose is a lyric redefining of a word whose meaning has been lost. Writing in 1852 of Fyodor Tyutchev, Turgenev suggested that the poet had created languages that would not die; what he wrote of the poet he could with justice claim for himself, as well: "Mr. Tyutchev can say to himself that he . . . has created forms of speech whose destiny is not to die; and for a true artist there is no greater reward than such knowledge" (V, 427).

There is a crucial sense in which Turgenev's attention to social discourse, hypocrisy, truth, and silence in *A Nest of Gentry* are parts of his own artistic credo, and form a fictive meditation on his own use of words. The relatedness of fiction and gossip is one of the implied assumptions of Turgenev's novel, as is the implicit "regeneration" of language through lyric and silence. M. Jules and Gedeonovsky, the novel's gossips, are narrators within the text: M. Jules's authorship of Varvara's life is a kind of inversion of Turgenev's authorship of Liza's. Both Gedeonovsky and M. Jules are storytellers; like the author of *A Nest of Gentry* they traffic in others' lives, implying truth by the shape they give to human experience. The parallels are, I think, conscious on Turgenev's part, and find confirmation in his other novels: in *Rudin*, Turgenev has Aleksandra Lipina draw an explicit analogy between storytelling and gossip:

> I'm sure that everything that you've said is true, that you haven't made anything up, but still, what an unfriendly light you've put it in! . . . You know, you can depict the life of the most splendid person in such colors—and mind me, without adding anything—that everyone will be horrified! Well that's also a kind of slander! (VI, 286–287)

Lipina's observation, and Turgenev's attention to gossip in *A Nest of Gentry*, reflect a concern on Turgenev's part that can be traced, in a historical sense, to his youthful acquaintance with the anarchist Bakunin. The latter's tendency to pry into others' lives was a form of intimate despotism; Rudin's affection for gossip—his passion for "defining" (*opredelenie*)—is Turgenev's development of Bakunin's trait. What Turgenev does with this, however, is not merely representational; he is not only being faithful to the historical model. In Rudin's gossip (the banal aspect of his eloquence) and in Jules's commercialization of intimacy, Turgenev is presenting questions about narration per se. What does it mean to tell the story of a life or of a moment? What is the position of the narrator in the tale—does he violate secrecy? Does he misrepresent the complexity of character? Does he simplify in order to control? To echo Lipina, how does the light cast on character predispose our judgment?

Turgenev uses theatricality in A Nest of Gentry as a figure for the inauthenticity and self-display of the gentry, and particularly in Varvara's case, as a metaphor for the conversion of every private emotion and event into public performance. The conversion of speech into script—as we witness in the drawing room melodrama of chapter 43—is one example of the deformation of intimate speech that is ubiquitous in Marya's world. Gedeonovsky's gossipy stories convert personal tragedy into entertainment, drained of understanding and compassion, yet pretending to moral judgment. Panshin's romance, written for Liza, assumes mutual affection and broadcasts it as self-reflective performance. M. Jules's gossip columns convert Varvara's life into fiction and fame. Finally, Marya feigns privacy and intimate speech, when there is in fact a spectator.

The implicit parallel of Turgenev's second novel is between the author himself and M. Jules: both writers convert private lives into popular commodities. Jules's role as a petty *deus ex machina* (it is his column that shapes Lavretsky's plot) is, perhaps, a bit of self-parody on Turgenev's part: the author controls his characters' fates. Turgenev's own implications thus anticipate Eikhenbaum's: Turgenev recognizes his own tale's affinity with society tales—a genre whose themes and discourse are built of gossip.[12] Society tales typically narrate the fates and fortunes of women in high society; they are fictionalized versions of gossip columns. As with gossip (either oral or printed), their appeal lies largely in their voyeuristic entrées to other lives; even satirical versions can still claim this attraction.

Gossip, speculation, and revision are the raw materials of Turgenev's novels (the same process is evident in *On the Eve*, where Insarov is anticipated in a series of "heroic" tales about him). Gossip, however, pretends only to entertain: Turgenev's narrative aims at wisdom and insight, at "truth jostling between phrase and pretense."

Turgenev distinguishes himself from these gossips in his vision and reticence, and in his separation of himself from worldly perspective. Turgenev narrates not only from within social discourse, but also from the solitary distance of the lyricist: his narrator can be both glib and contemplative. The carefully constructed double vision of Turgenev's plot gives us two versions of Lavretsky's story: the novel ends in elegy and lyric. The process of reading involves us in an education of the moral sight, so that we come at the ending to a vision that is tragic.

In a letter of 1859 to Evgeniya Lambert, Turgenev wrote of tragedy as ubiquitous and unperceived:

> Not long ago it struck me that there is something tragic in the fate of almost every person—only the tragic is often hidden from the person himself by the banal superficiality of life. Whoever remains on the surface (and many do), often doesn't suspect that he is the hero of a tragedy. . . . Here, for instance: all around me there are peaceful, quiet existences, but as soon as you look closely—the tragic is visible in everyone, either their own tragedy or one imposed by history or the development of a people. And then we are all destined to die. . . . What can you want that is more tragic?
> (P, III, 354)

Turgenev's statement returns us to that unsuspected world of William James's formulation, the world of unperceived, unspoken emotion that Turgenev excels in representing. *A Nest of Gentry* is Turgenev's narration of the close looking that perceives the unsuspected tragic; it is also a narration of those who do not suspect their involvement in the tragic. The vision of Marfa—a vision that we as readers are educated to share—perceives Lavretsky's tragedy, which is both "his own" and "imposed by history." The inhabitants of the novel's lower realm are, however, oblivious; Lavretsky's tragedy is hidden from them by the "banal superficiality of life." It is this banal surface that Gedeonovsky and M. Jules narrate; the lower world can only approximate the tragic in Marya's melodramatic scenes. Melodrama relishes the excess of gesture over substance: tragic emotion, which we know in Marfa's emblematic pietas, is substance that gesture only hints at, but cannot contain. Like *Rudin*, *A Nest of Gentry* recognizes that the novelist's craft exists in a continuum with forms of speech that pretend to lesser truths.[13] Gossip and salon talk are, however, broken in *A Nest of Gentry* by language that moves toward lyric. The epiphanies of silence in the novel are Turgenev's movements toward a purer speech, toward a language that does at last break free of phrase and pretense.

Chapter Three

HISTORY AND IDYLL IN *A NEST OF GENTRY*

"WHAT the soul is born to, God has given." *A Nest of Gentry* initially included as epigraph this quotation from Kirsha Danilov, an eighteenth-century compiler of ancient Russian heroic poems, whose work Turgenev read with great interest in the early 1850s. The extant manuscript of the novel, and its first journal edition, include the verse, which was omitted from subsequent Russian editions.[1] The epigraph nonetheless lingers as a paradoxical reminder of the substance of Turgenev's second novel—a novel as concerned with justice and retribution as it is with the more specific political issues of Turgenev's day. The providential determinism of Danilov's words—we get from God what we are born to—is the inscrutable truth against which Turgenev's hero Lavretsky must stumble. It is, elliptically, a foreshadowing of Turgenev's own narrative ending, one with which the reader must also contend in making sense of Turgenev's plot.

Turgenev abandoned the proverbial Danilov epigraph; he nonetheless retained within his text words that share with it an Old Testament concern with justice and reward. Anton, the house serf at Lavretsky's estate, is given to statements that echo Ecclesiastes, and comment on the absurdity of human suffering.[2] More importantly, Danilov's concerns are echoed in the compositions of the German musician Lemm, whose libretti are drawn from the Psalms. The Psalms, which are Lemm's favorite reading, meditate obsessively on justice and reward, on God's inscrutability and man's faith. In Lemm's biography, Turgenev introduces a story that narrates the worldly failure of a "righteous" man; it is a story that significantly parallels

Lavretsky's own. In Lemm's readings Turgenev reminds us of men's efforts to account for the apparent injustice of their lives. "Only the upright are righteous" (*Tol'ko praved-nye pravy*), Lemm's cantata proclaims; the ways of the world are, in *A Nest of Gentry*, lamentably far from such professions.

This novel takes us beyond the concerns of individual lives, however, toward both the polemics of Turgenev's age and the author's own more philosophical ruminations on the shapes of men's lives and of history. That the novel is connected to the debates on Russian history undertaken by Slavophiles and Westernizers—respective champions of Russian spirit and of Western intellect—has become one of the givens of criticism of the novel. Turgenev himself inserts into his text a dialogue of such positions in the salon argument of Panshin and Lavretsky in chapter 33; Pavel Annenkov, an early critic of the novel and close friend of the author, in fact pronounced the work "Slavophile" in spirit. While the cultural context of the novel's writing is not extraneous to my reading of it, I want nonetheless to examine in what follows, less that context than the structure of the novel, its plotting of idyll and history. I want to read the novel "intrinsically," but with some consciousness of the extra-textual positions that informed Turgenev's shaping of plot.

A Nest of Gentry engages history and religion, perhaps the two most central concerns of the Slavophiles. It does so, however, in a manner entirely integral to its own telling of a tale: it uses story, and the shaping of plot, to meditate on history. What this means is that in reading *A Nest of Gentry* I will attend to the shape of Turgenev's plot, taking that plot as both intentional and polemic: by interweaving idyll and history Turgenev engages in a dialogue both with the Slavophiles and with himself. If the novel has been called "Slavophile," it is because the idyllic longing of such lovers of Russia as Konstantin Aksakov was not wholly alien to Turgenev himself.

Turgenev drew the aphorism that initially served as epigram to the novel from a volume of Russian heroic poems (*byliny*) he had read in 1852, during the year of his enforced exile at Spasskoe, his country estate. It was a year he spent both in reading Russian history and in testing his own abilities as a novelist.[3] Throughout the year he corresponded frequently with both Aksakovs, father and son, who shared his interest in Russian history, but differed radically in their interpretation of it: "This winter I've spent a great deal of time studying Russian history and Russian antiquities; I've read through Sakharov, Tereshchenko, Snegiryov *e tutti quanti*. Kirsha Danilov particularly delighted me" (P, II, 59).

Turgenev was aware, however, that the opinions of his correspondents diverged significantly regarding these historical works: "All this led me to results nowhere near as comforting as it did you, my dear Konstantin Sergeevich." The particular nature of these less than comforting results, of the divergent interpretation, emerges from this and another of Turgenev's letters to the Aksakovs. What was at stake, in these letters, was not merely a collection of oral verse: at stake was a sense of the meaning of the Russian past—tragic for Turgenev, idyllic for Aksakov. In a letter of some months later, Turgenev again addresses the problem of their mutual views of Russian history:

I can deny neither history nor *one's own right to live*—a repulsive pretension—but I empathize with suffering. It is difficult to explain it all in a short letter. . . . But I know that this is precisely the point at which we diverge in our view of Russian life and Russian art—I see the tragic fate of a people [*plemeni*], a grand social drama, where you find the calm and refuge of epic [*gde Vy nakhodite uspokenie i pribezhishche eposa*]. (P, II, 72)

Turgenev's meditations here on history and genre go far beyond the debate at hand; they form the underpinnings of his great novels, in which "history" and "one's own right to live" are continually opposed. Turgenev's tragic irreconcilables—history and one's own right to live—are always at odds in his major novels: each of his first four novelistic heroes is caught between intimacy and the historical, between what they can control and what they cannot. Rudin, Insarov, and Bazarov are, all three, men with "world historical pretensions," whose heroic intentions collapse into the opposite longing: the desire merely to live. Bazarov's hubris is to attempt a denial of history's autonomy: "And as far as time goes—why should I depend on it? Better let it depend on me" (VIII, 226). Lavretsky, however, has no such pretensions, longing only for his "own right to live." For Turgenev, however, there is no retreat into either of these opposites: his heroes cannot be merely historical, nor can they be merely private.

Turgenev's comments to Konstantin Aksakov have a more particular significance in relation to his second novel, however. He locates their divergence of opinion at "precisely [this] point": "I see the tragic fate of a people, a grand social drama, where you find the calm and sanctuary of epic." This opposition of drama and epic is one that will underlie the plotting of A Nest of Gentry, for his second novel both narrates and aborts the idyllic calm of Russia's countryside, a calm that Turgenev names in his letter the "sanctuary of epic." "History" and "one's own right to live" are in fact the dynamic elements of A Nest of Gentry: Lavretsky's "longing to live" is expressed at the novel's center as his desire for rebirth, for Liza, for a life of sanctuary and calm. The "history" of Turgenev's novel is that force that prevents such desire and such idyll. A Nest of Gentry aborts idyllic calm and shelter, returning its hero to history, to the consequences of his and his country's past. Much of the novel's power nonetheless derives from the love and longing with which Turgenev was able to narrate idyllic life denied.

In Lavretsky's plot Turgenev developed what he found "hard to express in a short letter": the tragic fate of a man whose life is marred (and martyred) by history. Turgenev's novel thus addressed, in narrative form, those issues that underlay the polemics of his day. His novel suggests that the Slavophiles' fundamental assumption was of man's freedom from the past—an assumption Turgenev could not share. Beyond that, however, he also sought redemption for his martyred hero, a redemption found neither in history nor in God, but in contemplative perception. In this he remains true to the older oral wisdom of Danilov and the Psalmist. Lavretsky is, in this novel, bound by the past; his creator nonetheless seeks his freedom—not in history, however, but in poetry, in a move that is quintessentially Turgenevan. What Turgenev cannot establish (or hope for) in history, he can cherish in art: his novel is, finally, a celebration of the spirit in poetry, if not in the world.

Turgenev's letters to Konstantin Aksakov essentially conflate aesthetic and historical categories. Genres are ways of interpreting the past; the men diverge both "in our view of Russian life and Russian art." Aksakov himself had plotted Russian history in a "comedy" written in 1851, "Prince Lupovitsky." Aksakov wrote Turgenev of the play in 1852; Turgenev responded by reporting he had heard good things of the work—but hadn't expected a *comedy* from Aksakov: "I'll confess, I didn't expect a *comedy* from you" (P, II, 60).

Aksakov's "comedy" was published only some years later, in 1856—the year when Turgenev first conceived of *A Nest of Gentry*.[4] There is no direct evidence that Turgenev read the work—though the plot of his own novel, and its return to issues associated with earlier polemics, allow us to think he may have had *Lupovitsky* in mind in conceiving his own version of the return of an educated, Europeanized Russian to Mother Russia.[5]

Aksakov's play tells the story of an educated Russian who returns from Europe to his estate—filled with good intentions and preconceived notions about helping the peasantry and bettering their lot. In reality, however, it is *he* who is educated by the peasants: his homecoming is a discovery of wisdom, health, and virtue (and of peasant

society [the *mir*] as an ideal form of social organization)—
a revelation that it is he who is rejuvenated rather than
they. Aksakov's plot brings the hero back from Europe to
Russia—and discovers the "calm and sanctuary of epic" in
the world of the peasantry. The play obviously derives
from Slavophile historiography—but it is interesting precisely in its shaping of historiography as plot. The Slavophile plot is what Turgenev subsumes in his own narrative—giving it, however, a different ending.

A willingness on Turgenev's part to use narrative as historical allegory is apparent both in *A Nest of Gentry* and in
Smoke—the latter a novel that functions in many ways as a
satirical inversion of the earlier work. Both novels explicitly address problems of freedom and historical design—
though *Smoke* is concerned with the temptations of
"Slavic" irrationality, while *A Nest of Gentry* addresses the
temptations of the ahistorical pastoral. In both novels, the
author constructs plots that are both historiosophical and
didactic; the plots convey interpretations of Russian history that claim truth as historical reading and as foundation for personal behavior. Lavretsky's longing to escape
the past, and Varvara's sudden return, thus function in
Turgenev's novel as didactic structure, counseling the
inescapability of history, its presence as a form of fate. The
"return of the past" in *Smoke* is similarly associated with a
woman, Irina, but figures in that novel as an irruption of
the disorder and chaos that recur in Russian history. Both
novels project personal plot as emblematic of larger historical design; Turgenev's own structure claims the authority
of a different—tragic—view of Russia's past.

In a much-quoted letter of 1877 to a young woman
writer, E. V. Lvovaya, Turgenev insisted that one must
"write in order to tell a tale, and not to prove a point"
(*"scribitur ad narrandum, non ad probandum"*) (P, XII, 64).
Turgenev's own antipathy to tendentious art is evident in
his novels, in his qualified attitudes toward "heroes" of
progress—as in his quarrels with reductively political critics. The advice of the elder artist oversimplifies, how-

ever—for in his own narrative Turgenev did, in fact, engage in "proving." His argumentative methods are more subtle than some; his novels are nonetheless polemic, as is perhaps all narrative.[6]

A Nest of Gentry is shaped by two narrative movements, one progressive, the other a movement of return, which in their interaction suggest opposing historical and religious visions of Russia's destiny. The ostensible simplicity of Turgenev's narrative structure is in fact belied by a plot that reshapes chronology: the narrative of A Nest of Gentry sets the stage for Lavretsky's return to his native land, inserting his genealogy as an interruption of the narrative. This inversion calls attention to the counter-movements of the novel: the one movement heads out of Russia, and is narrated as progressive, frustrated enlightenment. This is the narrative of history in the novel, the inexorable, autonomous movement of time forward, a movement from which Turgenev will grant no escape. The other movement is one of return, both geographic and temporal: Lavretsky's initial return to Russia and Vasilevskoe, and his ultimate contemplative return in memory to the past. The first return—the plot of idyllic retreat—is for Turgenev illusory; the second return—of memory and art—is transcendent and free.

Turgenev's linking of such novelistic structure to visions of history and religion is suggested in his text's allusions to narrative prototypes drawn from religious tradition. Each of these movements of Turgenev's novel echoes in its structure a religious narrative. The novel's historical plot takes its shape from the recorded life of a martyr to history. The Slavophile idyll at the novel's center, the hero's return to Russia, is grounded in archetypal imagery of resurrection. Historical chronology and the attempt to break out of that time, to escape history, thus shape Turgenev's novel and his polemic.

The chronology of Lavretsky's life is grounded in his naming: Fyodor Lavretsky is a modern martyr, a historicized namesake of Theodore Stratilatus. The birth of Turgenev's hero is announced in *A Nest of Gentry* in a letter to his father, who is in Europe at the time of his son's birth: "[Pestov] congratulated Ivan Petrovich on the birth of a son, come to this world in the village of Pokrovskoe the 20th of August 1807, and named Fyodor in honor of the Holy martyr Theodore Stratilatus" (VII, 155). Like nearly all Russian children of his day, the boy is named after a saint: what was conventional in Russian society nonetheless becomes significant in Turgenev's text, a naming of the boy's fate that is borne out by his life. To recall the Danilov quote with which I began: Lavretsky is born to the name of a martyr, and it is the life of suffering that God will give him.[7]

The religious model of a martyr's sufferings, of which the account (*stradaniia*) of Theodore Stratilatus is representative, narrates the refusal of a believer to renounce his faith, a refusal for which he suffers.[8] In a world as yet incompletely Christianized, the martyr suffers for a faith that is alien to the society around him. These narratives traditionally focus on moments of suffering, emphasizing the martyr's strength during the ordeal, and his faith in God. The consciousness that his acts repeat those of other martyrs, and ultimately of Christ, endows his sufferings with meaning; the individual is transfigured in the communion of the suffering, certain of righteousness and of God's presence with him.[9]

If we take seriously Turgenev's naming of Lavretsky after a martyr, we must recognize in his novel a redefining of the term. In a novel like *The Idiot*, Dostoevsky places an essentially religious figure in a secular, fallen world; Turgenev's approach differs significantly. The "idiot" Myshkin retains features of a traditional saintly figure; Lavretsky does not. Dostoevsky plots the failures of holiness;[10] Turgenev plots the reality of martyrdom—a martyrdom that, however, differs radically from the religious archetype. Lavretsky is not a religious figure; it is the *absence* of a religious framework that makes the posing of his fate so radical. Turgenev names his hero after a religious figure, delivers him up to spiritual suffering, but deprives him of community and certainty of his suffering's significance. Lavretsky *is* a martyr, but to history. The fact that his martyrdom occurs outside of traditional faith deprives Lavretsky of the consolations available to Liza, who views their fate as providential. Turgenev's own plot will, however, offer other, nonprovidential, consolations for apparently meaningless suffering.

Lavretsky's fantasy of rebirth lies in its idyllic center; his martyrdom is bound to the novel's historical plot. The historical plot of *A Nest of Gentry* begins in the separate narrative genealogy of the hero, a biographical temporality that stretches from the hero's childhood to his final solitude. Lavretsky's childhood is recounted as part of a broader, continuous story, the record of Russian society in the eighteenth and early nineteenth centuries. Turgenev narrates that history as a chronicle of artifice that masks violence; the fathers' superficial efforts at Europeanization leave more fundamental power in feminine hands. Lavretsky's father returns to his estate after years in Europe, outraged at the "absence of system." His own introduction of order, however, is superficial: "New furnishings from Moscow appeared . . . they added a subscript to the family coat of arms: 'In recto virtus'. . . . In reality, Glafira's power in no way diminished" (VII, 160). Hypocrisy and domestic power are, in Turgenev's rendering, social forms of darker deceits; the moral history of the Russian elite emerges from his pen as a sequence of alternating fashions that returns, rather than advances forward. Russian history is cyclical, not progressive. The enlightenment pretensions of Lavretsky's father issue in the old man's literal blindness, a return to darkness that will haunt the son throughout his life. All apparent movement forward masks actual return; this failure of progressive temporality haunts the novel, both as history and as biography.

Into this chronicle of Russia's gentry Turgenev sets the life of his hero. Lavretsky's spiritual genesis is rendered symbolically in the account of his reading the book of *Sym-*

bols and Emblems, a book significant to Turgenev's novel both as a translation of European culture into Russia, and as the text that initiates Lavretsky's first attempt at leaving Russia's darkness behind.

> He used to sit in the corner with his *Emblems*,—he sits . . . he sits; in the low room it smells of geranium, a single tallow candle burns dimly, a cricket chirps monotonously, a small wall clock ticks hurriedly on the wall, a mouse furtively scrapes and gnaws behind the wallpaper, and three old maids, like the Fates, silently and hastily move their knitting needles, the shadows from their hands sometimes run about, sometimes hover strangely in the half-darkness, and strange, similarly half-darkened thoughts swarm in the child's head. (VII, 162)[11]

The scene of Lavretsky's reading of the Emblem book is itself emblematic of the world into which the boy is born, and of the process of escape. Turgenev represents Lavretsky's childhood here as enclosure in darkness and stasis, an arid womb that is a figurative tomb, as well. The monotony of this place is felt as well as represented, in the lengthy, repetitive periods of Turgenev's prose; the room in which the Fates sit is described as silent, still, unchanging. Turgenev's image is both historical and mythic, both a provincial enclosure and the prison of Fate.

In the larger plot, the enclosure and darkness within which Lavretsky's spinsters sit will repeatedly reclaim the hero in his efforts at liberation. The boy's desires for education are frustrated by his blind father's irrational anger (VII, 165); his movement toward light on his father's death culminates in marriage to Varvara, and a cuckolding that reawakens in Lavretsky the "peasant" (*muzhik*) (VII, 175).[12] Lavretsky's final movement toward Liza is aborted by Varvara's return, her parodic resurrection; Liza, image of virginal light and spirit toward which Lavretsky reached, is finally immured in monastic enclosure.

Turgenev renders enlightenment at times thematically (Lavretsky's longing for education), at times symbolically (as in Lavretsky's garden contemplation of Liza's veiled white light), but the figurative dynamic is always the same. Lavretsky's attempts to enter into, or grasp, light, are always frustrated. Varvara's return chains her husband to a deed committed in blindness; Liza's profession of vows removes the novel's virginal ideal from the world into the monastic "beyond."

Enlightenment and enclosure accompany Lavretsky's story as a repeated narrative figure of movement and frustration. The genesis of this narrative figure lies in the scene of the boy's reading: in a dark room, the boy reads a book that awakens his imagination. "Fedya looked at these drawings; they were all known to him down to the smallest details; some of them, always the same ones, set him to pondering and awakened his imagination" (VII, 161).[13] The scene of reading narrates freedom within enclosure; the boy is liberated in imagination even while he is physically contained. The ambiguity of such liberation is, however, implicit in the boy's "blindness" to the symbols' meaning. The pictures that fascinate him show cupids and bears, oblique visual references to a future fate he cannot as yet know. As obvious as these images' connection to the older man's amorous blunders is the implied qualification of this scene of enlightenment: the boy escapes his spinster Fates imaginatively, but his reading will not prevent a tragic mistake.

The darkness of childhood that binds Lavretsky fatally to Varvara is then embodied in this wife, who returns—a figure all in black—to frustrate Lavretsky's longing to marry Liza. In the love scene between Lavretsky and Liza in the Kalitin garden, Turgenev again emphasizes enlightenment and enclosure: his hero reaches toward light (here embodied by Liza), and is unwittingly entrapped in enclosed space. Lavretsky comes to the Kalitin garden at night, finding his way there as if by chance (VII, 235). His silent waiting in the garden is represented as a contemplation of light ("A candle burned in Liza's room behind a white curtain. Lavretsky sat down on the wooden bench

. . . and began watching . . . Liza's window"—VII, 235);
when Liza comes to the threshold Lavretsky emerges from
darkness and reaches toward Liza, his icon of light. After
their confession of love, however, Lavretsky returns to the
gate he had found open upon entering, only to find it
locked. He must jump over the wicket to leave; it is at this
moment that he says to himself, as in an incantation of
oblivion: "What has passed, dark phantom, disappear [*Is-
chezni, proshedshee, temnyi prizrak*]" (VII, 237).

The narrative irony of this scene lies precisely in the fact
that Lavretsky's "dark phantom," his past in the person of
Varvara, is even at that moment returning to him. The architectural detail of the locked gate functions in Turgenev's narrative as a symbolic reiteration of the hero's con-
tainment, his frustrated efforts to break free of an
enclosing past. The reaching toward light, toward enlightenment, is enclosed in a darkness that is fateful. The gate
through which Lavretsky and Liza might be united is fore-
closed. If, in the economy of plot, "jumping over the
wicket" can be construed as divorce—as the overcoming
of obstacles to union—it is a turn Turgenev's plot does not
take. Black-clad Varvara, the dark past, returns; virgin
spirit and light are entombed in monastic silence.

Turgenev's final figure of enclosure in the novel is, om-
inously, the monastery. The darkness and silence of Lavretsky's boyhood room are echoed in Turgenev's representation of Liza's monastic enclosure—a world that is
also characterized by silence and invisibility. Turgenev's
culmination of his plot with a return to enclosure unites,
at novel's end, historical and religious plots. The historical
plot brings Lavretsky to worldly solitude; Liza's ending is
a fundamentally religious resolution.

Turgenev's plotting of history in A Nest of Gentry thus
employs, repeatedly, figures of enlightenment and enclosure, and a historical darkness that appears inescapable.
Russian history in A Nest of Gentry is plotted as a series of
movements toward light, followed by descents into darkness. This historical plot is the novel's tale of martyrdom,
the tale of the sufferings of spirit in history. Movement to-

ward liberation is always aborted. It is in the second of Turgenev's narrative movements—in his representation of idyllic retreat—that the novel seeks a liberation that history will not grant. In traveling to Vasilevskoe—his country estate, and a world associated with the past—Lavretsky enters the Russia of the Slavophiles, a world untouched by the tragedy and darkness of Turgenev's other Russian past. It is in the novel's central section that Turgenev describes an idyll of retreat from the world, Lavretsky's movement from historical Russia into a country that exists outside history.

In an essay of 1847 (which for reasons of censorship was not published until 1883), Konstantin Aksakov gave succinct expression to the Slavophiles' historical thinking:

> Our past is not gone, it follows us. The past of Russia now lives with the common people and is preserved in them. Therefore, it is not a question of return to what has ceased to possess life, to what has passed, but to what is now living, that which exists and which has merely been deprived of a place in our social life and of a full manifestation. Such a return is possible and necessary.[14]

The past is not gone, nor is it a force to be feared: the past is a place, and for Aksakov and the Slavophiles, it was a place that promised regeneration for the Europeanized elite. Temporal divisions exist spatially in post-Petrine Russia: the idyllic past is still present, to be found in the peasant village.

It is this spatial representation of temporality that Turgenev plots in Lavretsky's journey to Vasilevskoe; in journeying to his estate, Turgenev's hero enters a place provisionally free of Varvara, Paris, and deception. The cart ride of chapter 18 is a journey in memory, during which images from Lavretsky's personal past coalesce with historical images:

> His thoughts slowly wandered; their outlines were as unclear and vague as the outlines of those high clouds, which also seemed to wander. He remembered his childhood, he

remembered his mother, how she lay dying, how they brought him to her and how, as she pressed her head to his chest, she almost started to weep over him, but she glanced at Glafira Petrovna—and was silent. . . . Once again images of the past rose up unhurriedly, flowed up into his soul, growing mixed and confused with other images. For God knows what reason, Lavretsky started to think of Robert Peel . . . about French history . . . about how he would have won a battle, had he been a general. (VII, 183–184)

This confusion of images marks the imaginative boundary that Lavretsky crosses in returning to his estate. What Turgenev shapes for us is Lavretsky's journey from the historical into the intimate, a realm freed of the constraints of the larger world beyond. Robert Peel and the French Revolution are history writ large; the world to which Lavretsky comes is apparently untouched by time. Thus Glafira Petrovna's house is unchanged: "Everything in the house remained as it had been" (VII, 185). "On the corner of the portrait there hung a wreath of dusty immortelles" (VII, 186). "Glafira Petrovna's estate hadn't yet managed to grow wild, but it already seemed submerged in that quiet slumber slept by everything on earth spared human, agitated infection" (VII, 188).

In entering Vasilevskoe, Lavretsky enters one of Turgenev's "charmed circles," a realm untouched by history and immersed in nature; he enters a world that will seem to offer rebirth and release from his past. When Lavretsky's friend Mikhalevich comes to Vasilevskoe, he quotes the last quatrain of a poem he has composed:

I have given myself to new feelings with all my heart,
I have become like a child in spirit:
And I burned everything to which I bowed down,
And bowed down to everything I once burned.

(VII, 201)

To become a child again; to be done with the past; to be reborn: Mikhalevich's verses state explicitly the pretensions of Lavretsky's stay at Vasilevskoe. The hero's immersion in nature in chapter 20 brings him to the symbolic goal of the journey begun in chapter 1—a journey that moves, significantly, through the home of Marya and Marfa. These two women are, in biblical narrative, sisters of Lazarus, the man Jesus raised from the dead. Lavretsky comes home to his symbolic rebirth through their portals.[15] His own immersion in nature, in chapter 20, is a metaphorical baptism, the moment of rebirth in Turgenev's novel. Turgenev's procedure is to describe his hero's rebirth, and then to challenge its possibility in the broader flow of history.

On the second day after his arrival at Vasilevskoe, Lavretsky rises early, talks briefly to the peasant elder, and once he has returned to the house, descends "into a kind of peaceful enthrallment, which he didn't leave all day" (VII, 189). The movement of immersion and rebirth is apparent in two senses in this section of Turgenev's narrative: in its imagery and in Lavretsky's resolve to mark a new beginning in his life, to break with his past. Turgenev's hero hopes to draw from his vision of peasant community the rule for his own existence, to learn to plow his furrow without haste: "Let it calm me, and prepare me to know how to act without haste" (VII, 190). Beneath these consciously articulated intentions, however, Turgenev narrates a symbolic return to the womb of nature, Lavretsky's spiritual rebirth in the motherland. The imagery of the chapter stresses enclosure, fluidity, silence; Turgenev draws on the archaic, powerful image of damp mother earth (*mat' syra zemlia*), portraying his hero as sunk back into a state of sensory acuity, in which sense of self is dissolved in the connectedness with the surrounding world. "He sat under the window, motionless, and it was as though he was listening to the stream of quiet life that encircled him, to the sparse sounds of country life. . . . What strength all around, what health in this inert quiet . . . quiet embraced him on all sides" (VII, 189–190).

The imagery of Turgenev's description traces his hero's

descent into a nature that is moist and circular, a fluid "bottom" in which he is enclosed, from where his perceptions are aural, at once intense and disjointed: he hears the humming of a bee, snatches of conversation lifted from their context. The imagery of quiet and enclosure is insistent; it is a silence that is dead and without will. Lavretsky sees the world from a radically different perspective, from a still bottom so far beneath the moving clouds that we almost feel he has shrunk, or receded into earth. The effect is one of perspective: he experiences the silent, the minute, with such acuteness that the alienation of what is distant is heightened. The clouds above, directed and dynamic, are images of a kind of life—a life of hurry and waste—that he has, for now, left behind. Enclosed in the heavy silence, which he experiences as slow, protective fluidity, Lavretsky has an epiphany of Russia—the homeland, the mother earth.

Turgenev traces in this scene an imaginative descent into enclosure that lies at the heart of all rituals of rebirth.[16] Descent into fluidity and the womb are retained symbolically in the rite of Roman Catholic baptism—where the baptismal font is named the "womb of the church" (*uterus ecclesiae*).[17] The agent of rebirth for Lavretsky is not, however, religious but natural; the imagery is not orthodox but archaic, mythic. The religious counterpart of this mythic rebirth occurs in Lavretsky's love for Liza, Turgenev's icon of purity and spirit. There are two agents of rebirth in Lavretsky's idyll at Vasilevskoe: the earth itself, dark and fecund, the embracing womb of maternal nature; and Liza, the icon of spirit and light. Turgenev's narrative draws on two powerful feminine images in depicting Lavretsky's rebirth, images that are deeply embedded in Western tradition and consciousness. His narrative, however, draws on those feminine symbols in their Russian variants; it is the Russianness of the earth and of Liza that Turgenev's plot underlines, thus emphasizing the particular and polemical nature of his usage. If Paris is associated, in Turgenev's novel, with the prostitution of self and spirit, a journey into a hypocritical void, Russia, on the other hand, is associated even in idealization with enclosure: with the womb and the monastery.

Lavretsky comes to repeat Mikhalevich's verses; after one of his conversations with Liza, Turgenev's hero rides home thinking of her, and these verses come to his mind: "And I burned everything to which I bowed down,/And bowed down to everything I once burned" (VII, 213). Turgenev indicates, with this echo, Lavretsky's still unconscious, unarticulated love for Liza, a love that will blossom with the false news of Varvara's death. Lavretsky's repetition of Mikhalevich's verses makes explicit the connection between love for Liza and renunciation of the past; Liza's love will make Lavretsky "a child" again.

The circularity of mythic plot, implicit in Lavretsky's return to Vasilevskoe and childhood, is sacrificed in Turgenev's plot to the linearity of history. Varvara's return to Russia parodically echoes both Lavretsky's return and the theme of rebirth (she had, after all, "died" in M. Jules's column), and returns Lavretsky to the chronology begun at his birth. History, and historical time, triumph in Turgenev's plot; Lavretsky's idyll is sacrificed. Turgenev's novel thus plots the "sufferings" alluded to in his letter to Aksakov: "I cannot deny either history or *one's own right to live*—a repulsive pretension—but I empathize with its suffering" (P, II, 72). What distinguishes Turgenev's emplotted martyrdom from the religious model—as from the ideological variants—is its emphasis on inner experience and its unwillingness to justify. The significance of suffering implicit in the religious tradition is withdrawn; Turgenev is similarly unwilling to replace religious with historical teleology.

If Lavretsky is a martyr, he is a martyr to a history that is dark, which has no transfiguration at its center. Lavretsky's pain is private, and modern: it does not lift him from the course of history and time, but condemns him to it. There is no repetition of a central act that confirms timelessness. Christ's suffering is followed by rebirth into eternity, a sequence that becomes the paradigmatic transformation of all martyrdoms. Lavretsky's suffering and "rebirth" are resolutely historical: they occur exclusively within a linear pattern of chronology. It is Liza alone in the novel who makes the passage from history into a veiled eternity. Thus, if the narrative paradigm of Christ's Passion has suffering followed by resurrection, Lavretsky's story traces suffering—rebirth—and suffering again. The longing for the past to disappear is a desire for an end of chronos and a beginning of kairos, a time of blessedness. Lavretsky's kairos is pastoral, not Christian, and is aborted by the return of a past that will not disappear.[18]

The freedom from history that Lavretsky seeks in *A Nest of Gentry* is denied him: this is the source of his suffering. Instead, Turgenev seems to offer his hero another sort of freedom—the freedom of inner life, art, and wisdom. Lavretsky's longing for the past to disappear takes on historical and philosophical dimensions when he and Panshin debate Russia's future; his flight from the past, and Russia's (or the Slavophiles') desire for freedom from her history, are interwoven both emotionally and rhetorically. "Lavretsky insisted on the youth and independence of Russia" (VII, 232). To assert Russia's youth is to assert her freedom, her unburdened state, the ability to choose without looking back. It is such a choice that Lavretsky wants to be able to make, and in defeating his hero's will to freedom Turgenev destroys the Slavophiles' pretensions as he has constructed them in his novel. The union of Liza and Lavretsky, of the motherland and the Europeanized elite, is impossible on the historical plane of Turgenev's novel— impossible because history (Varvara, Panshin, Marya—the whole legacy of Lavretsky's past) will not go away.

Turgenev's novel does not, however, assert historical inevitability, the triumph of necessity; instead, it offers a different, more hidden understanding of freedom and how it informs human life. That Lavretsky is unable to attain the freedom that he claims on hearing of Varvara's "death" does not consign him to slavery. The power that Varvara had once exercised over him she now directs toward Panshin: "He was enslaved by Varvara Pavlovna, enslaved: no other word can express her limitless, irrevocable, unanswered power over him" (VII, 287). The enslaved character of the novel's ending is this current lover, not Lavretsky, who is now free of Varvara's power. Lavretsky's liberation is nonetheless internal, not legal or tangible, and he must find peace with, and through, this hidden liberation. We recall the initiatory scene of the boy's efforts toward enlightenment: that blindness laid on Lavretsky in his youth has been lifted by experience. He has come through experience to understand the emblems of baroque passion, and is able at the end of his life finally *to see*. It is only at the end of this narrative that Lavretsky attains, at last, that inner state that permits him to look with equanimity at his life: "[Lavretsky] looked back on his life. It made him sad at heart, but he felt nothing either oppressive or deplorable: there were things to regret, but nothing to be ashamed of" (VII, 293).

As I have suggested in the preceding chapter, the ability to see distinguishes, in *A Nest of Gentry*, the upper and lower realms of the manor, the realm of tragedy and of farce. Marfa's moral righteousness, her ability to see things as they stand, removes her from the relativism and hypocrisy of Marya; Lavretsky's attentiveness, his moments of contemplative seeing, distinguish him from the active men (*deltsy*) of the novel—from Panshin and from Liza's father. Lavretsky's "blindness" when he fell in love with Varvara seems to find compensation in another kind of sight; Turgenev endows him with the attentive, absorbed, absorbing sight that was very much Turgenev's own.

The moments of contemplation in *A Nest of Gentry* constitute in fact a kind of second text within the novel, a narrative of lyric experience that traces a second, unseen chronology in Lavretsky's experience. Within Turgenev's historical narrative there are moments that allude to an experience within the historical that is, nonetheless, increasingly free of it, moments of contemplation that, while not religious, nonetheless grant Turgenev's hero a kind of freedom from temporality. As a boy, Lavretsky sits in a dark, musty room and looks at the book of baroque *emblemata*: the mysterious pictures, and the even more mysterious commentary, work in his imagination and carry him beyond the room, beyond the darkness. Lavretsky's contemplation of the picture book is his first step out of this world, the instigator of his search for liberation.

As a man, Lavretsky returns to Vasilevskoe, to his estate, to a Russia that is associated with maternity and childhood: he sits beneath an open window and watches the life around him—watches and listens until the activity of contemplation becomes an act of immersion. The journey out of the dark room—through his father's illness and death, the years of wandering in Europe, with Varvara and alone—brings him back to the place he had left, and back to another moment of contemplation. The first moment was "aesthetic," its object, European culture; the second is existential and Russian. From within the second moment Lavretsky surveys his life; within the moment of wholeness and immersion he perceives the possibility of a new beginning, a new rule and measure of life. He finds the wholeness of spirit and will that in Turgenev's text makes true choice possible. It is this second contemplation that is the beginning of Lavretsky's second passage, a passage associated with Liza.

Lavretsky's third and final contemplation comes at the novel's end, when he returns to the Kalitins', to the house in which he had loved Liza. An old man now, Lavretsky sits in the garden and bids farewell to the younger generation, wishing them freedom from all he has suffered. In this final contemplation, he is elegiac, and his vision is that of memory.

Lavretsky's first contemplation is aesthetic, and casts forward in time as a movement of liberation; his second is existential, a moment of contemplation in the present tense, in which time is full and sufficient unto itself. The final contemplation is also aesthetic, but it is now Lavretsky who is the poet, who is no longer mystified by obscure images but surveys and summons his past with equanimity. The temporality of this final contemplation is perfective, directed toward events that are ineluctably ended, irretrievable except in memory. From this vision comes a wisdom that the old can offer the young, a wisdom that Lavretsky seems to offer when he speaks of his "memories" (VII, 292). The younger generation within the garden seems not terribly interested in this wisdom: but we, a generation outside the garden, have already read and accepted it. The book we have read is, in some sense, the work of a sensibility closest to the aged Lavretsky, and in his final contemplation Lavretsky is closest to his author. It is in the epilogue that the hero's vision most approximates the author's, that the gap between them is the narrowest. The book has been written from the start by this elegiac contemplative; we are brought to his consciousness only at its end.

The three contemplative moments of *A Nest of Gentry* sketch the lyric time of Lavretsky's life: they are the real landmarks of his life, the true "events" of his biography. This inner lyric time of the novel coexists with its historic time, the paraphernalia of chronology that places Turgenev's novel in the life of society (its opening, the biographical digression, and the careful temporality of the epilogue). The novel's only other temporality is Liza's—and that is in fact a realm of timelessness, which begins only at the novel's end.

Within the novel, however, that genre that is bound and bred by time, Turgenev finds a liberation from temporality in the free movement of imagination. The lyric time of the novel—Lavretsky's contemplations—exists relative to historic time as a realm of freedom to one of necessity. When he participates in this time Lavretsky is free and blessed— in a way that neither Panshin nor Liza's father could ever be. Historic time in the novel is the realm of men's activity and work, for Lavretsky as well as for Panshin. The movement of this time is independent of us, inexorable, leading toward death: it is to this ultimate end that the narrator alludes in opening the novel ("[Marya's] husband, a former procuror for the region, in his time a renowned 'go-getter' . . . died ten years ago. . . . [Her] brother . . . mistreated both his sister and his aunt, until unexpected death placed a limit on his undertakings"—VII, 125). The effect of such details is to establish from the beginning a connection between certain forms of activity (bureaucratic, despotic) and a mortal end that makes human enterprise shrink in stature. The undertakings of the novel's active men are subject to this ultimate end, and in fact exist in sight of this finality (in the narrator's sight, that is—they themselves exist oblivious of it). What to Panshin and Kalitin is meaningful is rendered empty by this Ecclesiastian perspective of the end of all things. The life lived *merely* in activity is, from this other perspective, futile. It is a life governed by necessity and chronology, which threatens to turn men into beasts. It is this possibility of which Liza's father Kalitin seems dimly aware when he speaks of himself as a workhorse at a threshing machine: "He compared himself to a horse hitched to a threshing machine. 'How quickly my life's skipped by'—he murmured on his death-bed, with a bitter smile on his parched lips" (VII, 230). The "bitter smile" is telling: he dies in apparent recognition of mortality and futility, unmitigated by any Tolstoyan allusion to a vision of light.[19]

It is this enslavement to chronology that Lavretsky escapes—and escapes not through a reversal of history, but in his moments of contemplation. He is also subject to death, to the end that awaits the active men; but his life has, from within, been illuminated by love and perception—the qualities that Lemm, gropingly, tries to articulate as those that "justify" us: "Oh you stars, pure stars . . . you look down equally upon the just and the guilty . . . but only the pure of heart,—or something like that . . . understand you, or no—love you" (VII, 195). Lemm's awkward poetry is crucial to the novel's own ending, for it reverses standards of justification from outer to inner, from visible to hidden. The musician's own life is a chronicle of apparent failure: in the *plot* of his life he is unrewarded. His beloved Psalms, of course, promise ultimate recompense—a promise he seems to clutch with bitterness and uncertain faith. It is precisely such ultimate recompense that Turgenev does not promise: the spectacle of injustice with which the novel ends will not be compensated with ultimate rewards. Turgenev is concerned with historical, not divine, justice. Lemm's verses suggest that a martyred life is redeemed by inwardness—by the ability to see and to love. It is this redemption that is offered Lavretsky.

In his childhood reading, Lavretsky escapes darkness and the Fates; in his immersion in the motherland he escapes the bustle of "the world"; in his final elegiac meditation the aging man overcomes the tragedy that history has wrought. The liberation in any of these moments is a liberation of consciousness, and not of form. Formally, historically, the unrighteous triumph. But the final artistic victory is with the righteous—so that Turgenev's own novel stands as a moment of lyric time, an event that cannot be limited by its historical referents, but participates in that freedom that is of art and the human spirit.

Turgenev intended, in *A Nest of Gentry*, to project a vision of Russian history, and of the possibilities of an individual life within that history, divergent from the idyll of the Slavophiles. Throughout his life Turgenev was sober about the possibilities for true change in Russian society, as he was sober about the extent of human freedom to act in history. "Et puis, qui est-ce qui a dit que l'homme est destiné à être libre? L'histoire nous prouve le contraire" (P, I, 343).[20] Turgenev's rueful words to Pauline Viardot were motivated by the spectacle of the crushed Hungarian revolt of 1848; he followed them with Goethe's own sombre view of human freedom: "Der Mensch ist nicht geboren frei zu sein."[21]

The quote from Danilov with which Turgenev initially

prefaced *A Nest of Gentry* suggests a qualified view of human possibility, that we are born to limitation. That *given* comes in Turgenev not from God, however, but from history; his novel plots Russian temporality as darkness that contains liberation in structures of enclosure. The Slavophile idyll—the womb of nature, the monastic walls—is poeticized in *A Nest of Gentry*, but the deeper suggestion is of this idyll's affinity with other forms of entrapment.

A Nest of Gentry and *On the Eve*, Turgenev's third novel, were written just prior to momentous changes in Russian society—changes that promised at last to make possible a full break with a dark, embonded past. *A Nest of Gentry* is frequently read by critics as Turgenev's elegiac farewell to a disappearing Russia—and *On the Eve* as his affirmation of a future that would belong to a different breed of men and women.[22] Both novels are, indisputably, obsessed with change, shadowed by expectation of momentous event. The novels' sense of possibility, however, is oblique and hesitant—befitting a novelist who refused all comforts of idyll and teleology. Optimism and pessimism are, perhaps, reckless words—especially in speaking of Turgenev—and yet they are terms frequently used in speaking of both of these pre-emancipation works.[23] Turgenev's "optimism" in the ending of *A Nest of Gentry* is, at best, qualified, involving a denial of the historical wisdom of his own plot. Optimism in this novel is bought with a sacrifice of honesty—with a return to a celebration of idyll and historical freedom.

The social vision of Turgenev's epilogue is contained in his description of the Kalitin household, a household from which the elders have departed, where children now reign in a kind of blithe innocence. Marya Dmitrievna's house has been figuratively reborn; Turgenev's description is marked by allusions to the congruence of human and natural cycles, and by the vocabulary of marriage (VII, 288–289). Everything in the house has changed: "Everything in it had changed, everything was in harmony with the new inhabitants . . . the hours of breakfast, lunch, and dinner were muddled and blended together; as the neighbors put it, they had introduced 'unheard of ways' " (VII, 289). Everything has changed except the house itself—the structure of this world is the same, but it has been renewed, overthrown from within.

Turgenev's epilogue, in fact, transposes the idiosyncratic family of Marfa's room from the upper realm to the center—a transposition that, in the novel's terms, brings the locus of virtue and honesty into what was formerly Marya's salon. Shurochka—Marfa's orphan charge—has "grown up and become quite pretty": "This is the kind of young people who filled the walls of the Kalitin house with laughter and voices" (VII, 289). Marfa's denunciations of Gedeonovsky have become the children's laughter and pranks; the canary that was part of her family now sings in her salon. The language of sentimental hypocrisy has given way to the sound of birds, dogs, and children.

What Turgenev has done, in this ending, is to resolve his narrative with an idyllic vision: the optimism is ahistorical, implying the possibility of a decisive break with the past that the narrative did not allow. (As Lavretsky proclaims to the children: "You won't have to search as we did for direction, to struggle, fall and get up in darkness" —VII, 293.) The small utopia of Marfa's family state, where virtue is preserved at a heterogeneous tea party, becomes a larger utopia in this projection of the gentry house reborn. We may, however, accept Turgenev's epilogue as wishful thinking—his sense of what a future might look like—and still read its terms as meaningful. Dostoevsky called A Nest of Gentry "eternal" because of its presumed imagination of the reconciliation of Russian society with the "spirit and strength of the people." Such reconciliation crowns Crime and Punishment, but not A Nest of Gentry: Turgenev's ending implies renewal not through the common people but through a transformation of the gentry nest itself.[24] Turgenev's hopes lie here, as always, within the gentry enclave itself—which might find a way to reject the false legacies of Europeanization, and discover a higher truth already contained within itself. Here as before it is Marfa who is the novel's guardian spirit, the symbolic mother of its final transformation.

Turgenev significantly reworked the composition of his epilogue between manuscript and published versions, in a manner that suggests his thinking on the genre and justifications of the novel. In the manuscript, the enumeration of characters' fates is in a sequence reversed from the final version, and the final paragraph of the novel is omitted. Turgenev's original epilogue first traced Lavretsky's return to the Kalitin household, omitted the final monastery scene, and concluded the novel with a lengthy description of the fate of Varvara's father—who had fallen considerably in the world, and made his way by selling himself as a "considerable personage" at merchant weddings. The manuscript version ended as follows: "Evidently that's how it is in this world, everyone misses out on something" (VII, 378).

Turgenev's initial ending thus served as parodic closure, echoing the novel's intended epigraph with an epigrammatic reference to the "ways of the world." In ending with reference to imposture and marriage, Turgenev's first epilogue foregrounded the satiric intentions of the novel, giving the work the closure of comedy—ironically, of course. Varvara's father sells himself (at a bargain rate, since he lacks the requisite general's stars) to give importance to weddings: weddings, it is worth noting, are what is travestied in the novel's main plot.

Turgenev's final version of the novel's ending closes quite differently: with lyric, not travesty. His ending gives cursory attention to the novel's satiric cast, and closes— after the description of Lavretsky's elegiac visit—with the lyric passage into ineffability. This transposition of endings makes a substantial difference for the work of justification that Turgenev is about: the satiric intentions of the novel are left behind, and the final movement of the epilogue is "upward" and beyond. Turgenev's ending returns us figuratively to the higher, tragic stage, to the realm of unspokenness that is presumed beyond discourse.

In rejecting the manuscript ending for this final version, Turgenev traded travesties of weddings for weddings that bode harmony: the weddings of Shakespearean comedy, which connote the overcoming of dissonance, the institution of a just order. The couplings of the epilogue embrace only the younger generation, however: the final passages treat Lavretsky and Liza—the pair the plot promised to marry, and then held apart.

Turgenev gives to his "social drama," as he alluded in the letter to Aksakov, an ending that is both tragic and comic: the youthful joy of the children promises freedom from the past, Lavretsky's solitude and Liza's death to life remind us of bondage and martyrdom. Turgenev's hesitation between idyll and satire in writing the epilogue seems connected to deeper hesitations about Russia's future. Russia's radicals were less ambivalent: as the historian Franco Venturi has articulated their view, "The idyll—that is the enemy."[25] Turgenev's points of agreement with the radicals were very few; *A Nest of Gentry* nonetheless clearly registers his awareness of idyllic temptation. Historical plot in the novel is, I have suggested, linear; the idyllic return is aligned with impulses toward undifferentiated existence—the womblike enclosures of nature. Turgenev's narrative suggests that history in Russia is only tenuously progressive—always slipping back into enclosures of darkness. Pastoral tempts with reconciliations that are regressive. Reading allegorically, however, the idyll of the epilogue differs significantly from the idyll of Vasilevskoe: human rhythms are patterned here on nature's, but the structures of society, the architecture of culture, are intact.

Chapter Four

ON THE EVE AND THE SIRENS OF STASIS

À propos des anciens, je me propose d'aller l'un de
ces jours sur une des îles avec l'*Odysée* et d'y rester
un temps indéfini.

(P, I, 309)[1]

AT THE center of Turgenev's third novel, *On the Eve*, all of
the novel's major characters—Insarov, Elena, various
friends, Elena's mother—make an excursion to the Tsaritsyno ponds. Their day in this landscaped country includes
an hour or so spent on a boat, an hour of idleness when
they drift over absolutely still depths. During this boat
ride, Zoya—one of the novel's sillier characters—sings "Le
lac," Lamartine's poem set to music by Niedermeyer. In
the middle of Turgenev's novel about "heroism" and heroic passage, there is a moment of absolute stillness, an
echo of a text that is about transience and regret. The
poem Zoya sings is about the longing to stop time, and the
impossibility of doing that; it is a poem "fallacious" in its
assumptions of human and natural conjunctions. Lamartine's lyric pervades this moment of Turgenev's text, as it
does much of the narratorial consciousness of the novel.
There is, however, a deeper pervasion in Turgenev's text,
not by the verse alone but by the longing that motivates it:
Turgenev's third novel is suffused with the elegist's longing to abort passage, to rest in perception and end the various divisions of human life. The "eve" of Turgenev's title
is as much a boundary of death and stillness as it is one of
revolutionary change.

The possibility that *On the Eve* is as much about poetry
as it is about heroism, or that it represents aesthetic and

mortal stasis as much as it does dynamic intention, is not one that critics have tended to entertain. The novel is more typically read as Turgenev's capitulation to the enthusiasms of the late 1850s and his country's expectations of reform, with a hero and heroine who of all of Turgenev's characters come closest to embodying the antique meaning of those terms: Insarov the revolutionary hero (Bulgarian, not Russian, for reasons that have long absorbed critics) and Elena (an equally revolutionary heroine, whose radical behavior elicited both condemnation and imitation[2]) are representatives of the "new people" so eagerly awaited by midcentury radicals.[3] The novel, in this reading, significantly breaks with the lyricism of its predecessor, *A Nest of Gentry*, and is most purely definitive of the Turgenev novel in its attention to issues of historical and social concern. If *On the Eve* is regarded as the most dated of Turgenev's major novels, it is perhaps because it has been regarded as most deeply embedded in the concerns of his day, the least redeemed by other, more universal issues.

My intent in this essay is, perhaps, to redeem the novel by suggesting that it *is* quintessentially Turgenevan, and as "lyric" as its predecessor; I will focus, however, less on the novel's characters than on the author's shaping of plot and modulation of narrative tone—for it is in these qualities that I see the essentially Turgenevan character of the work. Turgenev's novel plots dynamic heroism, in a setting particularized and insistent on context. That same novel is informed, however, by lyrical passages that reshape its heroic plot, and make Insarov's heroic journey a voyage into inertia and death. Turgenev's novel appropriates the problems of Lamartine's poem—transience, absence, death—but it also recovers and reclaims the lyricism of Turgenev's own beginnings as a writer. That Turgenev is a "lyric" or "poetic" realist is a firmly established assumption of our critical tradition.[4] What is less firmly established is the precise significance of this lyricism for his novels. To read *On the Eve* is to address this issue in a particularly direct manner. Turgenev's narrative emplots the longings of his lyric imagery; one aim of this essay is to see how that happens—how narrative both qualifies and claims lyric conceit.

There is a series of passages in *On the Eve* in which dialogue cedes to description, passages that come at structurally significant moments in the novel (at its beginning, center, and end; at the moment of Elena and Insarov's confession of love to one another). The narrator in these passages describes nature or the inner states of the characters, and adopts the voice of a poet, whose topics are lyric and elegiac. The passages can in fact be read as poems in prose—forerunners of the genre Turgenev was to practice in pure form at the end of his career—which "interrupt" the dynamism of plot.[5] These various passages are, moreover, linked in their language and imagery, in their thematic and function. They repeatedly articulate the conundrum of stasis and movement that the passages themselves represent in the text. These passages arrest the flow of plot; they are also *about* the desire to stop all movement, to attain and hold an ideal, static moment.

Idyllic, aesthetic stasis is the explicit theme of "Be Still!" (*Stoi!*), one of the *Poems in Prose* composed in 1879. In this short prose piece Turgenev expressed to Pauline Viardot his longing to capture and hold her image at the moment of inspiration. He describes the singer at the end of her song, when the last sound is dying on her lips; this moment is, for the poet, a moment in which the eternal is fleetingly visible:

> Be still! As I now see you—rest forever thus in my memory!
>
> This is she—mystery revealed, the mystery of poetry, life, love! This, *this* is immortality! There is no other immortality—nor need there be. In this moment you are immortal. (XIII, 195–196)

Like the poet of Keats's "Ode on a Grecian Urn," the narrator of Turgenev's poem longs to arrest time, and sees in this vision of art a vision of eternity. The significant difference lies, of course, in the object of attention: for Keats the image of eternity is itself an inert object depicting movement; for Turgenev, the secret of poetry, life, and love is revealed in music, in an art that is essentially temporal. The ephemerality of the glimpse of the eternal thus informs Turgenev's poem more radically than it does Keats's. Both singer and song are temporal; to implore them to "Be still!" is to implore their destruction. The stasis of the moment exists only on Turgenev's page, and in his memory.

This longing to arrest the flow of time, this sense of the ephemerality of perception, the qualified endurance of memory and art, is not a unique concern of the older Turgenev. It is apparent much earlier in Turgenev's writings, at the height of his work as a social novelist. "Asya," a novella written in 1857, is a work explicitly about loss and memory: in a narrative turn that Turgenev will repeat almost obsessively, the hero loses his beloved through failure of nerve, and is condemned to possess her only in memory. The themes of loss and remembrance are conveyed not merely in the novella's plot, however. "Asya" takes as its dominant metaphors the passage and flux of water, time, and identity, juxtaposing the motion of the Rhine with the still image of a tiny Madonna, who presides over the narrator's indeterminacies. The Madonna, like the beloved once she is lost, becomes the sole constant of the narrative.

Memory and art, permanence and loss, are thus the topics of "Asya," as of "Be Still!" "Asya," however, because of its narrative form and length, accomplishes something "Be Still!" does not: "Asya" plots the contrast of human change and aesthetic stasis. The passage of the narrator (and of the girl Asya) stand in marked and melancholy opposition to the aesthetic stillness of the holy statue. The loss of the beloved at the novella's end transforms her into permanence in much the same way as does Turgenev's later prose poem: the changeable heroine will "be still" only in memory or art.

"Be Still!" and "Asya" diverge both in period of writing
and in genre; nonetheless there is a significant continuity
between these works, as there is between them and *On the
Eve*. Turgenev's third novel was conceived in 1853–1854,
four years prior to the writing of "Asya";[6] the period of
the novel's creation thus overlaps with his creation of the
novella. The congruence of novel and novella, their mutual concern with temporality and persistence, depends
less on coincidence of creation than on Turgenev's own
persistent concern with the topic. To depict "the body and
pressure of time," as Turgenev claimed to have done, was
to depict temporality, to meditate on the loss and ephem-
era of human existence, as well as on its achievements. It
is this that Turgenev does in *On the Eve*, making his meditation all the more radical, because he takes as his plot the
dynamism of heroic aspiration. Heroic plot epitomizes
purposeful movement, the progress of the hero toward a
goal, the projection of will through time, into the world.[7]
Turgenev places into this plot moments that both represent and embody stasis and the collapse of movement—
but also, moments that value perception over action,
which glimpse the goal of human striving as perceived,
not won.

Henry James, writing of *On the Eve*, said that it "breathed
antiquity." The heroic plot of Turgenev's novel does in fact
echo, in more ways than one, a classical heroic narrative,
Virgil's *Aeneid*. Virgil served more than once as subtext for
Turgenev; in *On the Eve*, the Latin epic of the perilous journey toward statehood is echoed in the structuring of Insarov's plot, the imagination of his purpose, and in the representation of what endangers the hero's goals.[8] Aeneas
travels toward the founding of Rome, on a journey repeatedly imperiled by the feminine. It is Dido, Queen of Car-
thage, who most powerfully threatens the hero's intentions; the Homeric hero upon whom Virgil based his story
must also pass through the lyric temptation of the sirens,
women who would seduce the hero from his goal with

their lovely song.[9] The heroes of antiquity are tempted by both eros and song, temptations they each overcome. If, as James suggested, Turgenev's novel "breathes antiquity," it breathes decay as well, and a consciousness of mortality. Turgenev's Insarov is tempted by eros as the text itself is tempted by song: the midcentury Russian cannot affirm, as did his antique models, the triumph of heroic will.

The sirens of stasis enter Turgenev's novel in this chapter's opening scene in which a woman on a lake sings a beautiful song. "Le lac" is sung in *On the Eve* by Zoya, Elena's frivolous companion. Zoya enters the novel on the banks of the Moscow River, in chapter 2; the artist Shubin—who has just been discussing nymphs and mermaids (*rusalki*) with Bersenev—speaks of Zoya as "charming" (*ocharovatel'naia*) (VIII, 16). *Rusalki* are the Russians' water spirits, Slavic sisters of Greek sirens;[10] Zoya's "bewitching" performance at Tsaritsyno enacts the implications of Shubin's earlier, playful remarks: she charms her audience.[11] Zoya's singing of the Lamartine is an enchanted moment, a moment that overcomes the temporal and psychological differences of the novel. The company is lulled, for a moment, by a siren song.

The Lamartine poem that Zoya sings in chapter 15 of *On the Eve* is a classic of its genre, representative of extreme romantic elegiac pathos. Turgenev repeatedly avowed his dislike of Lamartine, usually in terms so undignified as to suggest Turgenev was wholly dismissive. Thus, in a description of two dogs in a café, Turgenev calls the one "doux, rêveur, paresseux et gourmand, nourri des lectures de Lamartine, insinuant et dédaigneux en même temps" (P, I, 314).[12] The tendency to think of Lamartine when describing animals surfaces again in Turgenev's mock-meditation on a barnyard rooster: "Ce que je prenais pour du courage en lui, ne serait-ce que l'impertinence d'un farceur qui sait bien qu'on plaisante et qui se fait payer sa peine? Oh! illusions! Voilà comme on vous perd. . . . Monsieur de Lamartine, venez me chanter ça" (P, I, 341).[13] Lamartine obviously embodied for Turgenev the false rhetoric, the "sick whimpering" (*khiloe khnykanie*) (P, III, 67) of romanticism; but Turgenev's relationship to Lamartine—as, more generally, to romanticism—is quite complex, a process of resistance that is still ongoing in the novels (and, arguably, throughout his artistic life).

Turgenev's use of the Lamartine poem in his third novel does not render the epistolary jibes insincere. He echoes "Le lac" as an exemplar of romantic rhetoric and of a certain body of ideas about flux and permanence. The literary reminiscences, and the epistolary disdain, suggest something of the particular tensions in Turgenev's prose between the romantic heritage and his "realism"—and, perhaps, demonstrate some of the irony and wit with which Turgenev fought off this enduring influence.

Both the language and assumptions of *Le lac* are central for *On the Eve*. The poem is an elegy, written as the lament of a lover returned to a place he had shared with his beloved. The lover—the elegiac "I"—addresses the lake, asking nature to join with him in memory of what is lost.

> O lac! l'année à peine a fini sa carrière,
> Et, près des flots chéris qu'elle devait revoir,
> Regarde! je viens seul m'asseoir sur cette pierre
> Où tu la vis s'asseoir!
> . . . .
> Un soir, t'en souvient-il? nous voguions en silence;
> On n'entendait au loin, sur l'onde et sous les cieux,
> Que le bruit des rameurs qui frappaient en cadence
> Tes flots harmonieux.[14]

Inserted into the poem are four stanzas that are those of the lost beloved: the lover recalls a song she had sung, in which she lamented the passing of time.

> "Ô temps! suspends ton vol; et vous, heures propices!
> "Suspendez votre cours:
> "Laissez-nous savourer les rapides délices
> "Des plus beaux de nos jours!

"Assez de malheureux ici-bas vous implorent,
    "Coulez, coulez pour eux;
"Prenez avec leurs jours les soins qui les dévorent,
    "Oubliez les heureux.

"Mais je demande en vain quelques moments encore,
    "Le temps m'échappe et fuit;
"Je dis à cette nuit: Sois plus lente; et l'aurore
    "Va dissiper la nuit.

"Aimons donc, aimons donc! de l'heure fugitive,
    "Hâtons-nous, jouissons!
"L'homme n'a point de port, le temps n'a point de rive;
    "Il coule, et nous passons!"[15]

At the end of this quatrain, the lover himself continues the bitter meditation on temporality and isolation:

Temps jaloux, se peut-il que ces moments d'ivresse,
Où l'amour à longs flots nous verse le bonheur,
S'envolent loin de nous de la même vitesse
Que les jours de malheur?[16]

The poem concludes with a lengthy statement of Ruskin's "pathetic fallacy"; it ends with a hyperbolic final entreaty to a supposedly sentient nature. This "fallacy" has of course informed the poem as a whole, in its frequent address to the lake. Within Lamartine's apparently naive stance there lies, however, a much darker recognition of silence and nothingness: "Éternité, néant, passé, sombres abîmes,/Que faites-vous des jours que vous engloutissez?"[17] Even the high romantic text exists with the consciousness of the emptiness of its aspirations; Turgenev's novel will exploit both those aspirations and the poem's darkness.

Niedermeyer's version of the Lamartine poem is sharply abridged, and begins with the poem's second stanza ("O lac! l'année à peine . . .")—the single line that Turgenev actually quotes. Lamartine's verse is present throughout this passage, however, lending its rhetoric to Turgenev's own prose. Zoya begins her song with a line that ends in ellipses; Turgenev's narrator continues in language that uses the romantic clichés of Lamartine's verse. What Zoya sings is not narrated; but the narrator's own words echo the romantic poet: "Every word echoed far into the woods; it seemed that there, too, someone was singing in a clear and mysterious voice, not human, but unearthly" (VIII, 72). The song of the beloved in "Le lac" is introduced by a similar perception of unearthly sound; in Lamartine, the words of the beloved emerge from a sequence of "accents inconnus," "échos," and the attentiveness of nature:

> Tout à coup des accents inconnus à la terre
> Du rivage charmé frappèrent les échos;
> Le flot fut attentif, et la voix qui m'est chère
> Laissa tomber ces mots . . .[18]

The "unearthly voice" of Turgenev itself echoes the romantic image (with the significant qualifier, "it seemed"); Turgenev's narrator points to the same congruence of human and unearthly sound, to the echo (*otzyv*) of a world that listens.

The passage in Turgenev's novel articulates a moment of many congruences: the congruence of the assembled company—who are, in the larger narrative, anything but united; the congruence of nature and spectator; the congruence of opposed elements within the natural scene itself. The chapter begins with the bustle and frenzy of preparation for the "partie de plaisir"; when they all come to Tsaritsyno, they are held together in contemplation of the lakes before them: "Everyone drank in the view for a long time, in silence; even Shubin grew quiet, even Zoya grew thoughtful. At last, in unison [*edinodushno*, literally, 'with single soul'], they all wanted to go boating" (VIII, 72). The water to which they rush "with single soul" is itself an image of divisions overcome, of movement ended: "Nowhere, not even at the shore, was there a swelling of waves or the whitening of foam; not even a ripple moved on the broad, even surface. It seemed as though a thickening mass of glass lay heavy and lucent in a huge font; the sky disappeared in its bottom, and bowery trees looked motionless into its transparent depths" (VIII, 71–72). When everyone is finally in the boat, and they pause for Zoya's song, Turgenev repeats an image of stasis, one that conflates human and natural resting: "The wet oars lifted in the air like wings, and so they rested, letting drops fall melodically, the boat floated on a bit and stopped, barely turning on the water, like a swan" (VIII, 72).

The images of circularity and unity in this passage articulate its central conceit: divisions are overcome. Nature is unified in a landscape that resolves oppositions (sky and lake) and makes distinctions invisible (glass, transparent); from the contemplation of unity Turgenev's characters move *into* what they have been watching—they climb into a boat and move into that stillness that has been compared to a font (*kupelo*), as though their immersion in water and song could herald their own renewal, their own baptism.

Turgenev's passage accomplishes what Lamartine's poem longs for—an abolition of time. Turgenev represents in prose the present tense that is, for Lamartine, lost and lamented. When Lamartine's beloved begs that time stop its flight and allow the savoring of the day's delights, she begs for what Turgenev's passage delivers. It delivers, of course, only briefly. Turgenev sets this moment in his narrative as present tense—thus without the regrets of elegiac perspective that come in the poem. The elegiac poignancy and irony of past tense is displaced in *On the Eve*, to be recovered in the novel's ending.

Turgenev counters pantheistic longings in this moment not with the bitter recognition of loss, but with an abrupt collapse of romantic rhetoric, a switch from sublimity to bathos that centers on the romantic echo (*otzyv*). Zoya's voice seems to evoke an unearthly response ("Every word echoed far into the woods"); the sentence that articulates this is immediately followed, however, by a very different sort of *otzyv*: "Every word echoed far into the woods. It

seemed that there, too, someone was singing in a clear
and mysterious voice, not human, but unearthly. When
Zoya finished, a loud *bravo* resounded from a shoreside
pavilion, out of which jumped several red-faced Germans
who had come to Tsaritsyno *on a spree* [*pokneipirovat'*]"
(VIII, 72–73).[19] The echo of sympathetic nature is followed
in Turgenev's narrative by the *bravo* of drunken Germans;
the beautiful illusion is broken, the lyric moment aborted,
the narrative begins again. These Germans are the same
drunken picnickers who will later affront Elena's mother,
and call forth Insarov's heroic deed when he throws one
of them into the lake. Turgenev's transition from pantheist
rhetoric to banality signals forward to an event of the narrative that will impel its movement. Insarov's action
(surely a parody of the truly heroic) will solidify his image
in Elena's eyes, and thereby contribute to their union. His
action is thus a constituent element in the dynamics of
plot—something the Tsaritsyno moment is not. The song
in the boat creates stillness and harmony; the banal echo
of the Germans is a return to time and passage, to difference and separation.

After this uproar Elena's mother orders the boat to
move, and the plot moves on. Uvar Ivanovich—one of the
novel's buffoons—entertains the company with his bird
calls, apparently also an example of congruence between
the human and natural worlds. This is already a retreat,
however, from the congruence imagined in Zoya's song.
A buffoon making his voice sound like a bird's is quite different from a voice from within nature that speaks to man.
Turgenev's narrative thus distances itself doubly from the
moment of static illusion, in two moments of parody: in
the German "echo" and in the buffoon's farcical "song."

The central conceits of this lyric passage—of human
conjunction and cessation of movement—occur again in a
passage which recounts Insarov and Elena's admission of
love to one another. Their meeting (by chance or by the
Gods?—the novel lacks the certainty of Virgil) during a
rainstorm, when Elena takes shelter in a roadside chapel,

culminates in their embrace, a submission to each other that language, Turgenev's narrator tells us, cannot convey. Turgenev's familiar topoi of ineffability are repeated here ("There was no need for him to tell her that he loved her. He was silent; she also had no need of words"—VIII, 93), leaving their concourse to be articulated by the narrator. The language that the narrator uses to speak of Elena and Insarov is language that recalls Lamartine and the still moment at Tsaritsyno. Their love is articulated as haven, as stillness, as congruence and blurring of distinctions.

> The quiet of blessedness, the quiet of untroubled haven, of a goal attained, that celestial quiet that gives even death both meaning and beauty, filled [Elena] entirely in a glorious wave [*bozhestvennoi volnoi*]. She longed for nothing, because she possessed everything. "Oh my brother, my friend, my dear one! . . ." her lips murmured, and she herself didn't know whose heart it was—his or hers—that beat so sweetly and melted in her breast. (VIII, 93–94)

From this lyrical description the narrative switches to a dialogue between Elena and Insarov that is their own articulation of union: Insarov explains to Elena the conditions of his life and journey, asks her if she understands, if she is willing to undertake it with him. Her answers are a litany of affirmative *I know*'s, her articulation of the indissolubility with Insarov she has just felt. That indissolubility—the conjunction (*soedinenie*) of two people—is, however, something Turgenev's novel questions, both in its final sundering of what here seems absolutely attained, and in the language with which the narrator articulates their union at its inception.

Turgenev's language articulates romantic union in this passage as immobility (*nevozmutimoi pristani, dostignutoi tseli*) and the absence of desire (*ona nichego ne zhelala*), obliquely likened to death. At the moment of union, the imagery of inertia and death already enfolds a still headstrong hero; the "untroubled haven" links the moment both with watery Tsaritsyno and with the final waters of

Insarov's death. Turgenev's language qualifies his hero's intentions even before his plot has destroyed them.

The "blessedness of untroubled haven" that the narrator ascribes to Elena and Insarov in their embrace is radically alien to the heroic undertaking: Insarov's plot is a striving toward a goal; he is held here in an embrace, in the quiet of the "goal attained." The narrator's imagery—which speaks of quiet as that which gives to death itself its meaning and beauty—points ahead to the end that will in fact be Insarov's: Turgenev's novel brings his hero not to Bulgaria but to final stasis, to the quiet of death. The lyric triumphs in Turgenev's novel—but it is a lyric that imagines stillness not only as bliss and haven, but as deathlike. The end of movement—what lyric strives for in *On the Eve*—is the end of life; Turgenev's rendering of inertia is always fraught with this ambivalence, caught between blessedness and mortality.

The association of stillness and death can in fact be found in the very opening of *On the Eve*, in a scene of contemplative talk that precedes the initiation of dramatic action in the novel. That scene takes place on the banks of the Moscow River, where Elena's two unworthy suitors, Shubin and Bersenev, debate art and philosophy. Like the opening conversations of *Rudin* and *A Nest of Gentry*, their dialogue explicitly introduces some of the novel's concerns: the conjunctions of man and nature, the capacity of love, art, and country to unite human beings. It also stands as a still beginning to the narrative, as a prose poem within the narrative dynamic of the text. The plot begins when they leave their space under the tree and walk along the river (classic image of passage) where they meet Zoya. Their dialogue under the linden tree is broken by the narrator's description of the place in which they sit: his imagery describes, but it also comments on, the quality of their repose.

> Beneath the linden it was cool and calm; the flies and bees that had flown into its shadowy circle seemed to buzz more

quietly; the clean short grass, emerald-color, without a touch of gold, didn't move; the tall stalks stood motionless, as though enchanted; as though enchanted, or dead, small clusters of green flowers hung on the lower branches of the linden. With each breath sweet fragrance pressed into the very depths of one's breast, but the breast eagerly breathed it in. In the distance, beyond the river, up to the horizon everything shone and burned; occasionally a light wind moved there, breaking and intensifying the glare; a radiant cloud of haze hovered above the earth. There was no sound of birds: they don't sing at times of intense heat; but grasshoppers were whirring everywhere, and it was pleasant to hear this fervent sound of life as one sat in the cool, at rest: it inclined to sleep, and awakened dreams. (VIII, 11)[20]

This passage begins Turgenev's novel in several ways—most pertinent to my discussion, however, is its imagination of a silent haven that engenders sleep and dreams, its likening of bewitchment and death ("as though enchanted, or dead"). Bewitchment and death are qualities in this novel of both love and art; this passage evokes the haven and stillness of art—of art that is a space of the imagination, freed from earthly time and movement. The reader of *On the Eve* figuratively rests beneath this tree, from under which he or she is brought to dreams. The imagery of this passage suggests that the lassitude of contemplation and discourse is a kind of enchantment—and that this enchantment bears the image of death. (We are dead to our world as we read.) This first imagination of contemplation connects the impulse of our reading to other longings for repose in the novel: to Insarov and Elena's embrace, to the still boat at Tsaritsyno. *On the Eve* repeats this representation of stillness at its ending, when it depicts Venice as a world in which beauty and youth descend into mortal stillness. When Insarov and Elena come at last to Venice, they come to a world that plays with all sense of difference and time, to a city that is the grand enchantress. We come, that is, to the fullness of that dream begun beneath the linden tree. Turgenev brings both Insarov and his readers to different kinds of stasis: to death (the world's only true stillness) and to contemplation of beauty—the immortality of perception that, in "Be Still!" Turgenev calls the only immortality that we have.

Venice, in Turgenev's rendering, is a dream—the harmonious dream of a young god (*stroinyi son molodogo boga*), both mysterious and bewitching. (In the first long passage describing the city Turgenev speaks of Venice as "magical," "enigmatic," "mysterious," "captivatingly strange" —VIII, 151.) The city is the apotheosis of Tsaritsyno's allusions, both natural and aesthetic, and Turgenev articulates again the overcoming of divisions (both temporal and visual) in a watery kingdom. The blurring of divisions are here, however, revealed as illusory; the city points toward death, not toward conjunctions and completion. Verdi's *La Traviata* is powerful for Elena and Insarov because it articulates Insarov's mortality ("Lascia mi vivere . . . morrir si giovane!" ["Let me live . . . to die so young!"] VIII, 155). It is an uncomfortable aesthetic identification of beauty, death, and youth of which Venice is itself the fullest emblem.[21]

The disappearing details of these Venetian palaces evoke the other disappearance of the novel's ending— Elena's and Insarov's. ("The details of ornament and the lines of windows and balconies seemed to disappear."— VII, 155.) It is, finally, in Venice that Elena dreams of Tsaritsyno—a dream that transfigures the illusions of that day into the deathly promises of Venice:

> She had a strange dream. It seemed to her that she was riding in a boat on Tsaritsyno pond with some kind of unknown people. They are silent and sit motionless, no one is rowing; the boat moves by itself. Elena isn't alarmed, but bored; she wants to know who these people are and why she is with them. She looks, and the pond is growing wider, the shorelines are falling away—it's no longer a pond, but a turbulent sea: huge, azure, silent waves rock the boat majes-

tically; something thunderous and terrible is rising from the depth; her unknown companions suddenly leap up, cry out, waving their hands. . . . Elena recognizes their faces: her father is among them. But some kind of white whirlwind descends on the waves . . . everything set to whirling and was confused.

Elena looks around her: as before everything around her is white; but it's snow, snow, never ending snow. And she's no longer in the boat, she's riding in a carriage, as if from Moscow; she's not alone: beside her there sits a little creature, wrapped in an old woman's coat. Elena looks closely: it's Katya, her poor friend. Elena grows alarmed: "Didn't she die?"—she thinks.

—Katya, where are we going?

Katya doesn't answer and muffles herself up in her tiny coat; she is freezing. Elena is also cold; she looks along the road: a city is visible in the distance through the clouds of snow. Tall white belfries with silver domes. . . . Katya, Katya, is that Moscow? No, thinks Elena, it's the Solovetsky monastery: there are lots and lots of small narrow cells there, like a beehive; it's airless there, and constricting,—Dmitry [Insarov] is locked up there. I have to free him . . . suddenly a yawning grey abyss opens up before her. The carriage is falling, Katya is laughing. Elena, Elena! cries a voice out of the abyss. (VIII, 162)

What has happened here is that Turgenev has brought to completion a lyric pattern begun in his opening chapter, so that Elena's dream is a condensation of the lyric meditations of the novel as a whole. Recognizable moments from the narrative are repeated and distorted, made figures not in a realistic sequential plot but in the delirious continuity of a dream. They are no longer connected by the contiguity of prose—as they are in their initial appearances—but by some other, oblique principle.

Elena's dream conflates the obsessive imagery of the novel's lyric passages—water, death, immobility—and creates its own plot, according to the logic of the unconscious. We can read Elena's dream as a manifestation of her guilt, as an imagistic outcry of conscience at succumbing to a passion which has sundered bonds with her parents, and will destroy her beloved.[22] But her dream refers to the logic of Turgenev's plot as much as to the heroine's unconscious. If lyric and narrative are, to a large degree, opposed in Turgenev's novel, Elena's dream replaces Insarov's heroic plot with a different narrative logic. It is the plot of this dream that is realized in Turgenev's novel, and not the aspirations of victory and liberation implicit in Insarov's heroism.

Insarov is greeted at the novel's opening (by Shubin—again making important statements as he jests) as *"Iroi!"*—that is, he is given his Greek name, called a hero in the antique mode, the embodiment of will and purpose. Turgenev's plot, however, dissolves that purpose, transforms Insarov from "Iroi" to "a man" ("He was a man [*chelovek on byl*]" says Shubin, quoting *Julius Caesar*—VII, 141).[23] Elena's dream is an imagistic statement of this transformation, articulating in dream the plot that, in *On the Eve* replaces the heroic: the journey of the novel is from harmony to oblivion, from the illusion of stillness to cell-like enclosures of death.

This transformation and subversion of the heroic happens both in plot and character: the *Iroi* of the novel's opening is held from the reader at an aesthetic distance appropriate to the epic. Insarov's raving during his illness, his mortal delirium, collapses all distance, brings the reader into the intimate formlessness of disease and death[24] (VIII, 117). The collapse of the heroic—which is narrated in Elena's dream—is begun with Insarov's ravings: like Elena, Insarov retells his story in the language of incoherence. This incoherence and formlessness is the radical opposite of Insarov's heroic form—even more radical than Shubin's parodic representation of the hero as Quixote:

He fell into a state of half-consciousness [*On vpal v zabyt'e*]. He lay on his back as though crushed, and suddenly he seemed to see something: someone above him is quietly laughing and murmuring; he opened his eyes with an effort, the light of the spent candle raked over him like a knife. . . . What is that? The old magistrate is in front of him, in a heavy silk bathrobe tied at the waist with foulard, the way he'd seen him the day before [*nakanune*] . . . "Karolina Fogelmeyer"—mumbles the toothless mouth. Insarov looks, and the old man grows wider, swells, grows, he's no longer a man—he's a tree. . . . Insarov must crawl along the steep branches. He holds on and falls chest-first onto a sharp rock, and Karolina Fogelmeyer squats like a street hawker, babbling "Little pies, little pies, little pies"—while somewhere else blood is flowing and sabers flash unbearably . . . Elena! . . . and everything disappeared into crimson chaos. (VIII, 117)

This passage marks a forgetting in a profound sense: Insarov "forgets" his heroic perfection and stasis, and falls into mortality (the Russian idiom [*on vpal v zabyt'e*] connects forgetting and the semi-consciousness of disease), a passage that his delirium narrates as submission to banality—to the magistrate to whom Insarov went for Elena's passport.[25] The passage repeats the title of the novel, *nakanune*; but the *nakanune* of this passage refers backward, not forward. The dream dissolves in disappearance and chaos. *Nakanune*, we note, is an adverbial form that refers to indeterminate temporality. Turgenev's novel begins with expectations that the plot, like the title, will move heroically forward, will refer to time in the future. That plot breaks, however; the hero "descends" into mortality, and his journey is toward formlessness, oblivion, disappearances (the first of which occurs in the conclusion of this delirium: "And everything disappeared into crimson chaos").

The heroic plot is given at novel's end to Elena—*she* is the one who journeys to Bulgaria, who embodies will and purpose.[26] Her heroism and purpose, however, are fundamentally qualified by what has come before—predominantly by the insights and recognitions Turgenev gives to his lyric passages. Elena is "heroic" at novel's end, but she is also touched by a consciousness of mortality of which the novel's first hero, Insarov, seemed unaware. The Lamartine poem of the novel's center returns in Turgenev's ending, recalled not for its pantheistic affirmations, but for its darker rhetoric, its recognition of absolute loss.

When Elena, in chapter 33, comes to her moment of despair—after she and Insarov have heard Verdi, and she realizes that Insarov's death is near—her despair touches on the illusions of congruence to which the earlier lyric passages had alluded: "What is the point of this beauty, of this sweet feeling of hope, what is the point of a reassuring awareness of close refuge, of faithful support, of immortal protection. . . . Can it be that we are alone . . . alone . . . while everywhere else, in all of these unattainable abysses and depths—everything, everything is alien to us?" (VIII, 156). The terms of Elena's meditation—beauty, refuge, support—are the terms of those lyric conjunctions that have echoed throughout Turgenev's narrative. The consciousness of death and division that haunted those conjunctions belonged to the narrator and to Turgenev, who resolved those moments in mortality and the prosaic. Here, however, that consciousness is Elena's: what had been an authorial skepticism becomes instead the heroine's, a transition that fundamentally qualifies the nature of "the heroic" at novel's end.

As in *Fathers and Children* Turgenev gives to a heroic figure meditations on radical human solitude and insignificance. It scarcely matters here that the heroic doubter is a woman; in *Fathers and Children* Bazarov will share attributes of both Insarov's and Elena's characters—his determination, her final hopelessness. Where Bazarov echoes Pascal, Elena voices the lament lurking in romantic pantheism.[27] Her thoughts echo the words of both lover and beloved in the Lamartine text at the center of the novel: "L'homme n'a point de port, le temps n'a point de rive;/Il coule, et nous passons!" . . . "Éternité, néant, passé,

sombres abîmes,/Que faites-vous des jours que vous engloutissez?''

Elena's despair is more absolute, however, because it
questions the rhetorical assumptions of Lamartine's pantheist—she cannot end by affirming, as he did, that nature
retains any memory of human passing. The conjunction of
souls promised in Elena and Insarov's embrace is likewise
undone in the novel's endings: Elena and Insarov are separated, not united. The word conjunction (*soedinenie*) in
fact becomes an object of complex play as an Italian doctor
pronounces Insarov's death: "The foreign gentleman is
dead—*of an aneurism, coupled with degeneration of the lungs*"
("Il signore forestiere e morto—*ot anevrizma, soedinennogo s
rasstroistvom legkikh*"). The final conjunction of the novel is
of two mortal illnesses. In a statement that itself joins two
languages, the doctor repeats one of the novel's cherished
words—Bersenev, after all, began *On the Eve* by meditating
on what unites men—in what seems a final dashing of illusions: there is no permanent union, save man's union
with death.

Lamartine salvages time past through memory. This cer-
titude that nature shares remembrance with the poet dissolves in Turgenev, but *On the Eve* seems to echo the very
question the romantic poses: "Hé quoi! n'en pourrons-
nous fixer au moins la trace [de nos amours]?/Quoi?
passés pour jamais? quoi! tout entier perdus?''[28] Turgenev's novel echoes this question both in voice and resolution. Bersenev, looking at Insarov's desk when the Bulgarian has fallen ill, wonders if all will be lost—"Is it possible
it will all disappear? [*Neuzheli vse ischeznet?*]'' (VIII, 119).
The departure of Elena and Insarov from Moscow is described as their disappearance (VIII, 148); it is the same
fate that awaits Elena at the end of the novel: "Neverthe-
less, Elena's trace [*sled*] disappeared forever and irrevoca-
bly, and no one knows if she's still alive, if she's hidden
away somewhere, or if the petty game of life has already
ended, as has her brief wandering, and death's turn has
come" (VIII, 166).

Critics who read the ending of *On the Eve* as heroic and affirmative ignore the indeterminacy of its conclusion, the oblique Shakespearean tone of this final reference to Elena.[29] Dmitry Pisarev, one of the more radical readers of the novel on its publication, recognized perhaps unwittingly the novel's indeterminate ending, although he didn't like it: "There is no answer to the natural question: did Elena find her hero in Insarov?"[30] There *is* no answer: the ending of the novel is oblivion—Insarov dies and Elena disappears, and the *trace* (Lamartine's "la trace" and Turgenev's "sled") of their lives is lost. Lamartine posits the retention of memory in nature; Turgenev, on the other hand, transfers the locus of memory from nature to history—it is history (Bulgaria) that would remember Elena—but her fate is shrouded in oblivion. The sole trace preserved is literary, the sole memory is the artist's.

Turgenev qualifies the heroic undertaking by bringing his final hero, Elena, to a consciousness of solitude and indeterminacy. The celebrated unions of the novel—of Insarov with his people, of Elena and Insarov—are dissolved; the epic memory that consecrates valor—the Homeric legacy, or the Bulgarian chronicles that Insarov is translating (itself a memorial act)—find no equivalent for Insarov's story. It is the lyricist in *On the Eve*—the contemplative beneath the linden tree, who sees enchantment and death as kindred—who authors Turgenev's plot.

The enclosures of *On the Eve* are equivocal, both desired and destructive. The embrace of Elena and Insarov is imaged as harbor (*pristan'*): it is harbor and enclosure (a shipwrecked coffin) that finally claims Insarov. Turgenev seems to make one final gesture toward Virgil in his ending. In the *Aeneid*, Dido begs the furies to avenge her loss after Aeneas has left her:

> . . . let him not, even so,
> Enjoy his kingdom or the life he longs for,
> But fall in battle before his time and lie
> Unburied on the sand.[31]

Aeneas escapes the woman's curse. The furies of Insarov and Elena's affection bring Turgenev's hero to this death: never entering the Bulgarian kingdom, his corpse is thrown up on Adriatic shores (VIII, 165). Love and art, Dido and the sirens are the seductresses of stasis in *On the Eve*—tempting heroic movement into a fullness and quiet that is enchanting (*ocharovatel'noe*), but dead (*mertvoe*).

The brief epilogue of Turgenev's novel ends with a description of Uvar Ivanovich that reiterates the stasis and contemplative stillness that have seduced the heroic plot. Uvar Ivanovich—a figure whom Shubin calls ironically the "strength of the black earth," "the choral principle"— ironic synecdoches for Russia—stares off into the distance: ". . . cast into the distance his enigmatic gaze" (VIII, 167). Shubin has just asked him the question that motivated the novel's most famous critical response: "Will we have people [like Insarov] as well?"—to which Nikolay Dobrolyubov, in his essay "When Will the Real Day Come?" answered: "We will." The question is, however—as always in Turgenev—left unanswered. He has, nonetheless—to borrow a Chekhovian phrase—posed the question properly. Uvar Ivanovich and, presumably, Russia have in no way changed: ". . . he alone hadn't changed in any way." If Uvar is the "chorus," the representative of the black earth that is Russia, he is a figure for a world that is timeless, unchanging, and immobile.

It is in this epilogue that Turgenev invites allegorical and historical reading: the spirit of stasis, of changelessness, is Russia's. The seductive stasis of eros and art finds its historical counterpart in this Russian colossus, whose enigmatic gaze reminds us that, for Turgenev, Russia was always a Sphinx. The heroic endeavor in *On the Eve* is confronted with powerful resistance that, in the body of the novel, Turgenev connects with eros and with song. Uvar's final contemplation casts this stasis as specifically national, suggesting that the defeat of movement and will is particularly Russian, connected to this changeless, silent force. Uvar's gaze also, however, returns us to the novel's beginning—to the dialogue beneath the linden tree, to Shubin and Bersenev who are also looking into the distance: "The one . . . looked thoughtfully into the distance . . . ; the other . . . also looked somewhere in the distance" (VIII, 7). Looking, Turgenev's particular form of lyric insight, encloses Insarov's heroic plot. Insarov's journey is not above us, as in epic, but lies within the poet's insight. Elena's final journey, then, is of a heroic figure who has submitted to lyric—who has "looked" into emptiness—and goes on.

ODINTSEVA'S BATH AND BAZAROV'S DOGS: THE DISMANTLING OF CULTURE IN *FATHERS AND CHILDREN*

"After Pushkin, Turgenev is perhaps the only genius of measure, and consequently, a genius of culture. For what is culture if not the fathoming, accumulation and preservation of that which is valued?"[1]

TURGENEV's fourth novel is particularly concerned with the structures of human lives—in a very literal sense: the rooms, houses, and gardens that Turgenev's characters inhabit reveal them, as they reveal something of Turgenev's own thought. Place in *Fathers and Children*—as in Turgenev's other work—reveals character, rather than defining it; the connection of character to surrounding space defies the merely allegorical. Pavel's study, Fenichka's sunny room, Odintseva's manor, all sketch the contours of Turgenev's world, and come to suggest, in *Fathers and Children*, ways of living with what lies outside, beyond domestic enclosure, beyond human enclave. The domestic structures of Turgenev's novel mark boundaries with the natural world; they come to figure culture in relationship with nature. When Bazarov throws open Odintseva's window "at once, with a crash," he performs an elemental gesture of violent opening, a gesture that is a figure for other openings, destructions of other barriers. This confrontation of manner and passion is central to Turgenev's novel—not only because it is the culmination (without consummation) of Bazarov's entry into Odintseva's world, the lower class transgression of gentry enclosures—but because it reveals how thinly culture veils something more elemental. The world of nature and the world of human culture are not merely contiguous for Turgenev: they inhabit the same space, the same person. The novel's fundamental problem is what peace men and women will find with their nature: which, as it turns out, is a problem both psychological and political—a problem of social organization as of personal restraint. If Turgenev's novel seems to watch so closely the *boundaries* of the human and natural worlds, it is because these boundaries—architectural, gestural, linguistic—suggest what is hidden even as they cloak it. Turgenev hints at a knowledge of what culture masks, and it is that knowledge that informs his own allegiances, his own restraint.

We have come to accept *Fathers and Children* as an "ideological" novel, as a novel of historical moment. The ideological confrontations of *Fathers and Children* are, of course, bound to the period of the novel's writing, to the years immediately prior to the 1861 Emancipation. The emergence of a radical intelligentsia, the alienation of older reformers from a class without their culture or their patience—these are the social and historical categories that typically frame an understanding of the work. Turgenev's novel is, indisputably, bound to that decisive moment in Russian history, emerging as it did from Turgenev's perceptions of society at a moment of critical import. The novel's bond to that moment lies not, however, in the mere representation of actors and types, but in its meditations on culture and violence.[2] *Fathers and Children* dramatizes an assault on culture, society, civilization; it imagines the confrontation of elemental power with the fragile forms of human life. The "politics" of Turgenev's novel—its political psychology—do not derive primarily from the ideological skirmishes of Bazarov and Pavel Kirsanov, although these scenes are important in their mapping of positions and rhetoric. The more fundamental clashes, and the more fundamental revelations, lie in non-polemical discourse—

in Bazarov's encounter with Odintseva, in Arkady's narrative of Pavel's past, in Bazarov's teasing of Arkady when
he first sees Odintseva. The deeper terrain of Turgenev's
novel is sexual: it is in the encounters of men and women
that Turgenev demonstrates the proximity of passion and
civility; it is here that he realigns his characters, here that
he endorses the deceptions of culture as necessary.[3]

It is the psychological insight of this novel that ultimately shapes its political resolve; the perception of human beings' precarious control over their passional nature
informs Turgenev's conservatism, his rejection of violence
and revolution. Turgenev will shape his novel largely in
terms of modified pastoral, not—as some historians of that
genre see it—in order to "naturalize" political relation-
ships, but because Turgenev's pastoral imagines an equilibrium of culture and nature, an equilibrium that revolution, like passion, destroys.[4] It is that equilibrium which
Turgenev cherishes—an equilibrium that is, in *Fathers and
Children*, adaptive rather than static. Turgenev's political
ideal (his ideal of the human community) is finally a social
elaboration of his aesthetic ideal, that contemplative equilibrium he reaches at the end of "Journey into the Woodland."[5]

At the end of this story, the narrator spends more than
an hour watching a beautiful emerald insect; he draws
from his watching an insight crucial to all of Turgenev's
work:

> Watching it, it suddenly seemed to me that I understood the
> life of nature, understood its significance—something un-
> questionable and clear, although still a mystery to many.
> Quiet and unhurried animation, a leisure and reserve of feel-
> ings and strength, an equilibrium of health in each separate
> being—that is the very foundation of nature, its unchanging
> law, that on which it stands and endures. Everything that
> breaks with that measure—beyond it or beneath it, it makes
> no difference—it rejects as unfitting. (VI, 69–70)

This perception of nature's restraint and equilibrium is something Turgenev's narrator comes to only after a difficult passage through darkness and a very different sort of nature. The story opens with a vision of nature as hostile, inhuman: there is no rule (either ethical or aesthetic) for human life in the massive, silent forest into which the narrator travels. Turgenev's initial vision is of a natural world that crushes the human: "The unchanging, gloomy forest is sullenly silent or makes a muffled howl—and at the sight of it the consciousness of our nothingness penetrates more deeply and irresistibly into the human heart" (VII, 51). The final vision of nature does not nullify the initial one; rather, the wisdom of restraint and equilibrium rests within the earlier consciousness—of a world from which all that is human may disappear without trace. The perceptions of nature as hostile and as model of equilibrium are not, then, contradictory—but complementary. It is *because* nature is alien that we must learn restraint—or we become agents of that very alien power that would destroy us all.

Turgenev returns to these concerns in "Enough," a meditative story published in 1865, in the passages of that work devoted to art and nature. Art here is not an imitation of nature—it is an *affront* to nature—for it aims at a continuity and longevity of human value that nature denies. Turgenev isolates art from human political actions—because Beauty is, for him, more absolute than political truth ("The Venus de Milo is, perhaps, more unquestionable than Roman law or the principles of '89")—but also, I think, because Turgenev perceives the ease with which political man becomes an agent of destruction: "It is true that people assist [nature] in its destructive work; but isn't the same elemental power, the power of nature, manifest in the barbarian's cudgel senselessly smashing the radiant brow of Apollo, in the bestial cries with which he threw Apelles' painting onto the fire?" Turgenev closes this passage, finally, with a cry of despair—in words that recall the initial passage of "Journey into the Woodland": "How can one hold firm against these heavy, coarse, endlessly and voicelessly [bezustanno] advancing waves, how finally can one believe in the significance and dignity of those transitory images that we shape from dust for the moment in darkness, on the edge of the abyss?" (IX, 120).

This anguished question is thrown out by a persona who has failed to find his way out of the "dark wood" as did his predecessor in "Journey." The persona of "Enough" is bereft of the final epiphany of meaning; in "Journey," the narrator emerges from despair into the company of peasants and their stories—for the narrator of "Enough," "the rest is silence." The terms of their despairs are nonetheless identical, as is their topography of embattled culture. The narrator of "Enough" imagines human creativity at the edge of an abyss, in darkness; the narrator of "Journey" has a kindred vision of the human, though he imagines not merely the realm of art, but of all human creativity. The imagery of "Journey" is gentler, but the topography is the same: the world created by human hands lies within a larger world that is alien. "He feels his solitude, his weakness, his incidental nature—and with hasty, hidden fear he turns to the small cares and tasks of life; he feels more at ease in this world that he himself has created, here he is at home, here he still dares to believe in his significance and strength" (VII, 51–52).

The narrator of "Journey" speaks of "small cares and tasks," the narrator of "Enough" speaks of the Venus de Milo—but in both cases the world imagined is one in which humans are creators, a world to which men and women give significance and meaning. It is a world in which they are at home, a world that *is* their home, because they have shaped it. The forest of "Journey" is alien but benign; the nature of "Enough" is violently destructive—but they are one in their elemental indifference.[6]

The topography of "Journey" and "Enough" are important for *Fathers and Children* because human creative and destructive urges are at the very center of that novel. The narrators of Turgenev's novels always turn from the glimpse of the alien wood to the places where men and women are at home: the estates of provincial Russia are those "worlds within worlds" where men and women make their peace with nature. What distinguishes *Fathers and Children*—and what makes it so much more than a novel of generations—is that Turgenev brings into his house of culture the force that would destroy it, Bazarov, whom Turgenev first imagined as emerging from the very depths of the earth: "I dreamt of a gloomy figure, wild and large, grown half out of the earth" (P, IV, 381). Like a figure from the *Metamorphoses*, Bazarov joins earth and the human, in an elemental and destructive transformation.

Turgenev's imagination of Bazarov as a figure suspended in metamorphosis entered deeply into the final narrative of *Fathers and Children*. There are two stories from Ovid that will linger in this novel: the first is the story of Actaeon, a tale of transgression and retribution that culminates in the hero's destruction. The second is the story of Baucis and Philemon—that pastoral couple who are emblematic in death, as in life, of simplicity, harmony, and endurance. These stories, and Turgenev's use of them, suggest that the human becomes "natural" in divergent ways: man may become brutal, and be destroyed; or he may live an ideal of harmony, and endure with the earth. Bazarov, Turgenev's transgressor, will "violate" the world to which he comes; Turgenev's novel will have that world endure.

Bazarov enters a world of pastoral and culture to unsettle it—which he does. The ultimate resolutions of the novel will restore those values that preceded him. Turgenev's restorations must be read, however, in light of the novel's revelations, which are in themselves trenchant and unsettling. This chapter examines revelations and resolutions in this novel, looking first at Turgenev's use of the pastoral in *Fathers and Children*, and then at the enclosures that sustain, and the encounters that threaten, the novel's imagined order.

Fathers and Children is repeatedly and insistently aware of a literary mode to which it seems problematically to belong: the pastoral. When Arkady, rising on the morning after his arrival at Bazarov's parents, is greeted by the elder Bazarov working in his garden, this retired army medic merely gives explicit articulation to themes and *topoi* less vocally present throughout the novel: "And as you can see, here I am—like some kind of Cincinnatus, digging out a bed for autumn turnips. . . . And it turns out that Jean-Jacques Rousseau is right. . . . I know you've grown used to luxury and pleasures, but even the great of this world won't disdain to spend a short time sheltered in a hut [*khizhina*]" (VIII, 318–319). The father at work in the garden is at once simple and literate—aware of his literary models without being burdened by this consciousness. To call oneself Cincinnatus is to recall the mythic figure who left his pastoral fields to serve his country—and, the task accomplished, returned to his home, eschewing civic fame and glory. And if Arkady and Bazarov—the "great ones of his world" have come to the parents' home as to a "modest hut," they follow the retreat of heroes to the pastoral oasis, a place apart where the epic plot is for a moment suspended.[7]

The most manifest emblem of the pastoral in Turgenev's novel is, of course, one of the central heroes—Arkady, whose name itself is evocative of the literary tradition.[8] Arkady's name bespeaks the classic topos of pastoral, the region of central Greece that, in Virgil, first became symbolic of idyllic rustic life. Similarly, Bazarov's parents—despite the father's reference to Cincinnatus—bring to mind the classic figures of what Rennato Poggioli has called "the pastoral of innocence," Baucis and Philemon.[9] Emblematic of hospitality, kindness, and conjugal peace, Ovid's couple enter Turgenev's novel as figures of rural simplicity and goodness—and as evidence of a kind of continuity the novel will want to embrace.

Turgenev's immediate Russian predecessor in the depiction of this classic pair was Nikolay Gogol, whose "Old

World Landowners" explicitly declares its pastoral model in drawing the landowners of the title: "If I were a painter and wanted to depict Philemon and Baucis on the canvas, I wouldn't have picked any original but them."[10] Turgenev himself returned to the couple—in a more parodic, but also more despairing vein—in his last novel, *Virgin Soil*: the eighteenth-century manor of Fomushka and Fimushka is given its pastoral title: "No 'novelty' penetrated the border of their 'oasis' [*Nikakoe 'novshestvo' ne pronikalo za granitsu ikh 'oazisa'*]" (XII, 126).

The emblems of classic pastoral enter Turgenev's novel in diverse and plentiful ways. They enter it, however, only to be modified by that novel's own complexity: *Fathers and Children* makes use of the pastoral, but it is not itself a pastoral. The novel is anchored as firmly in history as are all of Turgenev's novels. The setting of *Fathers and Children* is Russia in the summer of 1859, a moment that "marked the parting of the ways between reform and revolution."[11] The modifications of pastoral by history, the balancing of idyll against reality, are evident from the novel's opening, when pastoral and revolution are brought into sharp—if subtle—opposition.

Turgenev opens the novel with the scene of Kirsanov awaiting his son—a moment in which the narrator presents a brief story of the father's life. The section of this story that is crucial to me comes toward its close, as the narrator relates Nikolay's marriage and the birth of Arkady. The brief period of married happiness is introduced with references to the country and to Arkady—whose birth gives a name to that place that encloses the couple's life. The "country" where Arkady is born is an Arcadia— a seven-year idyll of conjugal bliss:

> Husband and wife lived very well and quietly: they were almost never apart, they read together, played the piano for four hands, sang duets; she planted flowers and kept an eye on the poultry yard, he occasionally went hunting and took care of the farm, while Arkady grew and grew—also well

and quietly. Ten years passed like a dream. In '47 Kirsanov's wife passed away. He barely withstood the blow, turned grey in several weeks; he was planning to go abroad in order to distract himself, if only a bit . . . but then '48 arrived. (VIII, 198)

The idyll of happiness is ended by death; the prose passage that narrates a "dream" closes with the year of revolution. Turgenev's ellipses are a kind of final, sobering boundary, a passing from the personal to the historical, from pastoral to revolution.

This narrative juxtaposition is crucial for *Fathers and Children,* for it suggests in miniature the novel's larger encounters. To resolve pastoral in death is already to modify the classic model; to allude to revolution in the context of pastoral is to bring together radically different visions of human activity and time.[12] These initiatory figures—pastoral, death, revolution—will be the novel's focal ones, though Turgenev rearranges their sequence. Turgenev's problematic closure significantly restates this initial bit of narrative logic. His pastoral is made "realistic" in its recognition of death: but the ominous initial sequence of pastoral, death, revolution is inverted in Turgenev's ending. Bazarov—the novel's 1848, its figure for revolution—comes first in Turgenev's closure: revolution, death, pastoral. The hero in revolt will submit to a larger order.

In alluding to the novel's ending, I make a rather broad leap across the novel's complexity: the sequence of the narrative will justify that reversal, and show how Turgenev inverts the tiny story of Kirsanov in his larger story of Bazarov. The novel opens, however, by announcing its own concerns; the shadow of death and revolution falls from the first.

The second extended allusion to pastoral in *Fathers and Children* comes in chapter 3, as the narrator describes the cart ride to the Kirsanovs' home. This is the novel's first lengthy piece of nature description—the reader's introduction to Russian Arcadia—and it is important in its dual referentiality, its evident placing of the narrative in history, even as it plays with a literary prototype. The initial modification of pastoral by death is here continued.

This passage is given as the perceptions and reflections of Arkady; the consciousness that sees is not the narrator's but one of the character's. Such rendering indirectly characterizes Arkady—for we learn that he is already fraught with a poet's bad consciousness, that he shares his father's lyric openness. The passage also, however, characterizes Russia: historical and natural Russia, Russia the work of men and Russia the gift of nature. Arkady's vision gives a double image, both ironic and redemptive. The irony emerges from his first long glance—a view of Russia in decay—which is framed by his own name: a name that of itself reproaches Russia with its failures.

> The places they were driving by couldn't be called picturesque. Field after field stretched to the very horizon, sometimes rising slightly, sometimes descending again; here and there small woods were visible, and winding ravines scattered with sparse low shrubbery, recalling to the eye their own image on old maps from Catherine's time. There were small streams with stripped banks, tiny ponds with narrow dams; villages with low huts beneath dark roofs that were often half fallen in, with walls of brushwood and yawning gates beside emptied threshing barns; churches, sometimes brick with peeling plaster, sometimes wooden with tilting crosses and ruined cemeteries. Arkady's heart tightened little by little. As if intentionally, the peasants they met with were all ragged, on wretched horses; roadside broom trees stood like beggars in rags, with peeling bark and broken branches; emaciated cows, rough-skinned as though gnawed to the bone, fed hungrily on the grass along the ditches. It seemed they'd only just torn free of some terrible, deadly claws—and amidst the beauty of a spring day arose the pale spectre of merciless, endless winter with its blizzards, frosts and snows, called up by the pathetic sight of debilitated animals. . . . "No,"—thought Arkady—"it's a

poor place, it strikes you neither with its plenty nor its in-
dustry; it mustn't, it mustn't stay that way, transformations
are essential . . . but how to bring them about, how to begin?" (VIII, 205)

What Arkady sees is not Arcadia but its opposite: a land
ruled by death and winter—a season unknown in classic
pastoral. Poverty is not, on the other hand, alien to pastoral; the ability to desire little is a virtue of the genre. Arkady, however, sees decrepitude, not poverty, as though
the simplicity of pastoral summer has fallen into decay.
The allusions to Arcadia serve only as sobering negatives:
this is not Arcadia, this is Russia; its emblem must be
change, not harmonious continuity; ". . . it mustn't, it
mustn't stay that way."

The second portion of what Arkady sees begins with a
change of season: ". . . spring came into its own." We
have moved from winter to spring, from naturalism to
pastoral—and from the human world to the world of nature. Arkady's second vision is of a world free of the human—here he sees neither meager ponds nor dilapidated
threshing barns, but only that which grows from the earth
without human intervention. "Arkady looked and looked,
and as little by little he relaxed, his thoughts disappeared. . . . He threw off his overcoat and looked at his
father so cheerfully, with such a boyish air, that his father
embraced him again" (VIII, 206). While the first paragraph
ended with an awareness of the desperate need for
change, the second ends with gestures of liberation and
renewal that occur, as if of themselves, through the
agency of nature. Arkady throws off his coat in a shedding
of the winter he has just seen; in feeling himself once more
a boy he can embrace his father.

The passage as a whole moves through a recognition of
historical reality, a posing of a terrible problem, to a pro-
visional resolution and reconciliation. Pastoral here seems
a way of forgetting what has just been seen, an exchange
of historical for natural truths. These two visions—of a

world that is fallen but also redemptive—are what Turgenev holds to in *Fathers and Children*. Redemptive nature does not, however, sanction oblivion; Turgenev's novel is full of the realities of midcentury Russia—Kirsanov's problems, the realignment of classes, intellectual ferment. The novel will, however, answer Arkady's question—"How to begin?"—in pastoral, not revolutionary terms. And pastoral, for Turgenev—as a category of thought, with implications beyond the merely aesthetic—involves a sense of how to reconcile history and nature, change and continuity.

Bazarov enters this novel as an embodiment of what aborts the widower Kirsanov's plans: 1848. Turgenev's allusion to the revolution of his lifetime—one he had witnessed—is not, I think, fortuitous. 1848 was the watershed year of European society in the nineteenth century, a year that even in its failures left the world changed. Turgenev's reaction to the revolutions of 1848 was never as violent as Herzen's, for Turgenev's initial sympathies were quite different. There is, nonetheless, in his writings about the period a recognition akin to Herzen's—though without the bitterness and "Slavophilism" of the latter's *Ends and Beginnings*.[13] In "Our People Sent Us" (*Nashi poslali*), Turgenev narrates the confusion of the June days, when the workers of Paris rose against the bourgeoisie; what emerges from his sketch is a patrician's recognition of a new class of men. In "Our People Sent Us" the workers are valiant—in "The Execution of Troppman" they are elemental and amoral; in both pieces they are alien, harbingers of a new world.

Bazarov is akin to these men of 1848 both in his class, his "otherness" for his patrician author, and in his radicalism. Much has been written, and contested, about Bazarov's ideology; Pumpiansky, in the important 1929 edition of Turgenev's works, contended that Turgenev set the novel in 1859, rather than later, in order to avoid portraying Bazarov as a revolutionary.[14] The Russian scholar goes on to criticize Bazarov's materialism—physiological, not historical—as incapable of sustaining revolutionary activity. His argument nonetheless ignores the insights of Turgenev's own text, which represents Bazarov as a figure of absolute revolt, a figure who *implied* revolution; Turgenev related Bazarov in correspondence to the rebel Pugachev, and in the novel itself to 1848.[15] It is perhaps worth remembering, in this context, that Turgenev's concern with 1848 is evidenced in another novel—*Rudin*—to which he returned just prior to the Reform. The epilogue to that novel, depicting Rudin's death on the barricades, was added in 1860; one wonders if Rudin and Bazarov were not linked in Turgenev's mind—with 1848 and with Bakunin, that apostle of destruction so intimately known by Turgenev. Arkady's question, "How to begin?"—a variant of Chernyshevsky's novelistic "What is to be Done?"—finds an implicit respondent in Bazarov. Bazarov's historical analogues may or may not have been found among the radicals of 1859, but Turgenev did not betray history in depicting his hero. He followed, rather, his intimations of consequence: that "physiological materialism" would breed another 1848. The implications of Bazarov's entry into the Kirsanov's decaying pastoral world are profound. It is to that entry—to encounters and implications—that I will now turn.

When Arkady and Bazarov retire to their bedrooms on the night of their arrival at the Kirsanovs', Bazarov makes a rueful comment on his room—a comment meant to stand as metonymically critical of the larger society: "There's an English washstand in my room, but the door won't lock. Still you've got to encourage them—English washstands, in other words, progress!" (VIII, 210). The appurtenances of health and comfort can be imported, but the basic structure is rickety—such seems to be Bazarov's intended criticism. But what follows his comment—the narrative description, Turgenev's own indirect commentary on the household—reads the details differently. Turgenev will, elsewhere in the novel, use domestic metaphors to describe the workings of society—as, for instance, when the narrator speaks of Kirsanov's new agrarian arrangements "creaking like homemade furniture made of raw wood" (VIII, 227). In the passage at hand the same rhetoric is evident—but with different implications for Bazarov and the narrator.

After Bazarov's comment, the narrator goes on to wander imaginatively through the Kirsanov household as it goes to sleep: from Arkady's bed (where the young man sleeps under a blanket made by his nurse's "beloved hands"), to Nikolay Kirsanov's room, to Pavel's study, and finally to Fenichka's quarters—where the chapter's final image is of an open door: "[Fenichka] looked toward the open door, from behind which was visible a child's crib, and where the even breathing of a sleeping child could be heard" (VIII, 211). The open door is here a virtue, not a fault; the narrator's free gaze finds narrative passage through all those doors that don't lock, and makes of that free passage an attribute of this world as of his consciousness. Between Bazarov's door that doesn't lock, and Fenichka's open door, the narrator creates a commodious enclosure where men and women, peasant and master, child and father live together. In a novel which meditates so carefully on the social structures that shape men's lives, this domestic space is an imagination of society—where classes and generations coexist in a structure of order and peace.

It is worth noting that the house is a new one, just built, and called—among other names—"New Settlement [*Novaia slobodka*]" (VIII, 207). It is not surprising, then, that on the morning after their arrival, it is Bazarov who is the first to leave this enclave of liberal openness and effort: "The next morning Bazarov awoke and left the house earlier than everyone else" (VIII, 211). The narrator goes on to detail Kirsanov's arrangements—a pond, two wells, new trees—but notes that they haven't "taken" too well, with one exception: "Only the arbor of lilac and acacia had grown in properly; they sometimes drank tea and had din-

ner there." I have translated Turgenev's *besedka* here as
"arbor." Its etymology is nonetheless clearly connected to
beseda and *besedovat'* "to converse"—thus pleasantly con-
flating season and pursuit: one drinks tea and talks *en plein
air* in a structure built for clement weather. This series of
descriptive details lends itself to allegoric reading of the
kind Turgenev's prose seems frequently to invite: in the
"New Settlement" which is Russia in the process of reform, there is much that has not yet taken root, that appears scrawny and lame. The *besedka*, however, icon of cultured discourse in the bosom of nature, is doing well.
Post-Nicholas Russia, regardless of the efficacy of eco-
nomic and social measures, is a freer place, where men
may speak more openly. This was in fact true—1859, the
time of the novel, *was* a period of gentry discourse about
Russia's future, a time when even Herzen could endorse
Alexander.[16] The novelistic allusion to this fact moves it,
however, from the realm of statement to that of hypothe-
sis: as with his imagined domestic peace, Turgenev is
imagining—and hoping—that the *besedka* will flower and
hold fast. There is, nonetheless, an ominous tenor to the
word, which the nineteenth-century lexicographer Dal'
defines as "any small, light and temporary construction
for protection."[17] The semantics of instability encroach
upon Turgenev's icon of civic dialogue.

This arbor will, of course, play a crucial, dramatic role in
the novel—most importantly, as the place where Bazarov
kisses Fenichka, glimpsed by Pavel. The summertime
structure remains, one of the emblems of Turgenev's civic
imagination, projecting, like the new Kirsanov house, an
ideal of human community. The essential trait of this ideal
is its openness, both to the natural world around it and to
the alien Bazarov. Two other domestic enclosures that Turgenev details in *Fathers and Children*—Pavel's study and
Odintseva's manor—diverge from Kirsanov's home in just
this element: both Pavel and Odintseva live shuttered
lives, where forms of enclosure have become structures of
willed repression. Turgenev uses repressive domiciles not

merely as forms of narrative contrast, but also as intimations of what lies behind and necessitates those shutters. It is in Turgenev's most "cultured" characters that the delicate boundaries of culture and passion are implied. Turgenev's arbor is a structure for summer, surrounded by domesticated nature. What both Pavel and Odintseva suggest is another kind of nature—neither vernal nor tame, which is restrained only by the elaborate rituals of their lives. Katya will later say to Arkady of Bazarov: "He's a predator but you and I are tame [*On khishchnyi, a my s vami ruchnye*]" (VIII, 365). One of the unsettling revelations of the novel—a revelation that jumbles categories of class—is that Bazarov has companions in his wildness: Pavel and Odintseva—who have chosen lives that Turgenev's *raznochinets* will not.

Arkady's first gesture in returning home is to throw off a constricting garment: constricting garments, however, are the very stuff of country life for his uncle Pavel. The "freedom of country life" (*svoboda derevenskoi zhizni*) is evidenced by his freely knotted tie, but his tight collars are "unrelenting": ". . . the tight collars of his shirt lay with their customary absence of mercy against his cleanshaven skin" (VIII, 215). Dress, like the rooms that men inhabit, both masks and reveals: Pavel is, throughout, a man of culture and conventions, in whom the natural is concealed, constricted, perhaps dead. Pavel's final intention in the novel is to go abroad—to Dresden or to Florence, until he dies: "I will go somewhere further away, to Dresden or Florence, and I'll live there until I croak [*budu tam zhit', poka okoleiu*]" (VIII, 363). The statement is eminently revealing of Pavel, both in the goals of his journey—cities of exquisite culture—and in his jarring use of the verb *okolet'* (a word used of animals—hence wholly stripped of the refinement that is otherwise Pavel's) to speak of his own death. His phrase combines icons of culture and distance with a word startling in its coarseness—Pavel's own combination of disdain and ironic bitterness about his material existence. What redeems Pavel, what makes him a sympathetic character—and one so crucial to Turgenev's intentions—is that we know that the nature he masks is passionate, perhaps *too* capable of love. Turgenev gives us Pavel's masks, but he also gives us Pavel's story.

Pavel's study—the room in which we see him alone—is an elegant and shuttered emblem of the man. Nikolay Kirsanov meditates in the arbor, where he submits to elegiac emotion and memories of pastoral, memories to which the narrator has full access (VIII, 250); Pavel Kirsanov meditates in his study—his thoughts meticulously hidden from us by the narrator. We guess, however—from Arkady's story—that those thoughts are of his beloved princess, of his youthful passion. The difference is an important one: Nikolay's pastoral breeds elegy, whereas Pavel's passion breeds his rituals of culture. Turgenev's story of Pavel's past motivates, and gives meaning to, what would otherwise seem heartless and dead.

Turgenev describes Pavel's study in a brief passage at the end of chapter 8—Pavel has just returned from Fenichka's quarters, where he asked her to buy green tea. The description of the study follows immediately on Pavel's own vision of a conjugal peace unknown to him: we move from Fenichka's jam jars on window sills to Pavel's heavy furniture and his final gesture of concealment: "Whether he wanted to hide from the very walls what transpired on his face, or for some other reason—in any case, he got up, unfastened the heavy window curtains, and once more threw himself onto the couch" (VIII, 233).

Pavel's study itself is a monument to the transformation of nature's materials into artifacts of culture: the fittings of this room suggest elegantly transmuted wildness, they allude to violence subdued. Pavel's walls are papered in a "wild color" (*dikogo tsveta*: the color is literally dark grey, but the archaism retains other connotations in Turgenev's context), a weapon of some sort hangs on a Persian carpet, the furniture is of walnut. Turgenev's description of a somewhat conventional gentleman's study holds in its very epithets a sense of what culture is about: a transformation of nature into the appurtenances of human lives. In other passages of domestic description, however, we are reminded of the human agents of this transformation: Arkady lies beneath a blanket made by his nurse's hands, Fenichka's room is cluttered with jars of jam she has made for Kirsanov. This sense of agency is however lost in Pavel's room, where the manicured aristocrat sits in an elegance that is alien even as it alludes to its occupant. The exotica of Pavel's room—the gun, the Persian carpet, a color whose name is wild—evoke a past he has hidden, his own encounter with the untamed.[18]

What is hidden here is revealed in chapter 7—in this ordered novel's own small narrative of chaos and disorder. Pavel's passion for Princess R. is a disruption of equilibrium that borders on madness; Pavel's story is in this sense the polar opposite of Kirsanov's idyll with his wife— a story of human emotions that are wild, and hence incommensurate with the pastoral.

We are told Pavel's story by Arkady, who embarks on his narrative in order to do his uncle "justice" (VIII, 221). What we discover is that within the carefully collared gentleman there lies a man capable of extreme passion, of submission to a woman whose image is "incomprehensible, almost without meaning" (*ètot neponiatnyi, pochti bessmyslenyi, no obaiatel'nyi obraz*) (VIII, 223). Translators of *Fathers and Children* have rendered *bessmyslennyi* as "vacant" and "absurd," as well as "meaningless," perhaps necessary compromises that suggest emptiness but that lose the emphatic marginality of the Russian: both the adverb almost (*pochti*) and the prefix *bes-* (without) bespeak the shadowy realm between sense and incoherence.[19] Pavel's story "explains" the man's own enigma by describing his enthrallment to an enigmatic woman. The "dying, flaring" blue flame that Pavel watches in solitude (VIII, 211) evokes, dimly, his own near-consumption in a passion that bordered on insanity: "He almost went mad [*chut' s uma ne soshel*]" (VIII, 223).

What is crucial here is Pavel's movement toward a point

beyond which lies true madness, incoherence, absence of all sense: where the almost meaningless becomes *truly* meaningless. Arkady's story is an intimation of what Pavel's rituals and collars hold in check. The man is an icon of civility, but also of passion, and the adverbs of approximation in his story—*chut'*, *pochti*—define a psychic boundary he has approached and from which he has retreated.

Turgenev narrates in Pavel's story an account of passion and near-madness in the past tense; the encounter of Odintseva and Bazarov will involve a similar looking beyond the boundaries of civil life, narrated here in present tense. After Bazarov's confession of love, Odintseva will look "beyond a certain point," only to see "emptiness, or formlessness" ("Beyond her she saw not the abyss, but emptiness . . . or formlessness [*uvidala za nei dazhe ne bezdnu, a pustotu . . . ili bezobrazie]*") (VIII, 300). The encounter with Odintseva marks the center—the hero's crisis—of *Fathers and Children*, but not because Turgenev trades ideology for romance, thereby "belittling" his hero. This encounter is at the novel's center because it renders dramatically, gesturally, with a subtlety more trenchant than verbal argument, the clash of civility and passion, of civilization and revolt, that Pavel and Bazarov debate in chapter 10. Like the story of Pavel's past, the encounter of Odintseva with Bazarov will mark the boundaries of culture with what lies beyond, will imaginatively dismantle a world secure in all its forms: of structure, speech, and sense.

When Arkady and Bazarov travel from the Kirsanovs' household to Odintseva's manor, they move from a world immersed in change and the preparations for change, to a world of order and immobility. Odintseva's house, like her life, is a model of absolute order, established by the dead husband whose spirit still presides. This woman's kingdom participates in Turgenev's allegorical topography as a world submitted to an authority that is absolute even in absence of its central figure: a husband who was old enough to be Odintseva's father. ("Odintsev, a rich man of forty-six or so, an eccentric, a hypochondriac, pudgy, difficult and bitter, but still neither stupid nor mean"— VIII, 270.) Odintseva's psychic and sensual retreats will be governed by this allegiance to an order both psychological and social. "Order visibly reigned in the house: everything was clean, there was a kind of decorous scent everywhere, as in ministerial receiving rooms" (VIII, 274). "Reigned" (*tsarstvoval*), decorous (*prilichnyi*), ministerial (*ministerskii*): Turgenev's description of Odintseva's home conflates politics and decorum in the novel's most extreme example of repression and constraint.

The order of Odintseva's house is not, of course, Nicholaevan, despite the references to royalty and bureaucracy. Even Bazarov can appreciate its benevolence, its gentle temporality:

> Time (as is well known) sometimes flies like a bird, at others creeps like a worm; but a man feels particularly fine when he doesn't even notice if it goes quickly or quietly. Arkady and Bazarov spent their fifteen days at Odintseva's in just such a manner. In part that was due to the order she maintained in both her house and her life. (VIII, 284)

Odintseva's justification of her insistence on routine is that, otherwise, one would perish of boredom: ". . . one mustn't live in a disorderly fashion in the country, boredom takes over" (VIII, 285). But Odintseva's own sense of something foregone, of the price paid for relief from boredom, is hinted at in a passage that describes this woman whom the narrator calls a "rather strange being" (VIII, 282).

This passage—which was a later addition to the initial manuscript of *Fathers and Children*[20]—describes Odintseva as a woman of paradox, for whom wealth and comfort have prevented knowledge of passion, whose mind is "at once ardent and indifferent." Turgenev's description of Odintseva—his narrative of her childhood, her father's dissipation and her own resolve not to sink, impoverished, into provincial banality—are interesting and important, because they give a sense of this woman who can say to Bazarov: "You know, you're the same as I am" (VIII, 292).

Turgenev begins this description of Odintseva with an enumeration of her unresolved longings, her lack of passion; he ends with a description of her in a moment of solitude—bathing—that both in allusions and rhetoric defies the decorum that Odintseva so meticulously observes. Turgenev's narrator, voyeurlike, watches Odintseva in a moment of literal nakedness; the narrator's own transgression, however, is matched by Odintseva's. Odintseva and Turgenev's narrator manage, in this scene, both to observe propriety and to suggest its violation; both point to an erotic imagination that was, in Turgenev's day, far more heavily veiled than in ours.[21]

Odintseva, says the narrator, was carried by her imagination "even beyond the boundaries of what is considered acceptable by the laws of conventional morality" (VIII, 283). The narrator goes on to say that, even at such moments, her blood remained quiet in her "charmingly slender and quiet body." The narrator then proceeds—in a rhetorical sequence that links his own imagination to Odintseva's—to imagine her stepping out of a "sweet-smelling bath, all warm and languorous" (VIII, 283). It is at such moments, the narrator tells us, that Odintseva thinks of life's worthlessness and sorrow—but she is immediately checked in her thoughts by a cold draft from a half-open window. From Odintseva's own illicit imagination, via a reference to this woman's beautiful body, the narrator has come to a vision of her bathing. Both imagination and vision carry us beyond the "permitted"; Odintseva's thoughts are a hidden defiance of the decorous house in which she lives, an erotic transgression she has no will to sustain. The narrator's vision of her is also, however, a transgression—an unveiling of a woman whose body is so much admired by the novel's men. What is so striking about this passage is how nearly it suggests Turgenev's identity with his heroine: his willingness to allude to a transgression that remains hidden, his final resolve not to break with decorum in favor of passion. Turgenev plays here with the boundaries of decorum, in a manner that both points to the seductive beyond, and holds to the compromises of convention. Odintseva's flirtation with the forbidden will be repeated dramatically in her encounter with Bazarov; the narrator's own ambiguous position—between decorum and erotic curiosity—is played out in an earlier dialogue between Arkady and Bazarov, when they first meet Odintseva.

The young men's dialogue takes place at the governor's ball, where Arkady has spent an hour in conversation with Odintseva. Arkady is both enchanted and aware that Odintseva is fairly oblivious of him; as she leaves him to go to dinner, they follow the conventions of polite society—she turns to give him one last glance, he bows slightly—but Turgenev modifies this ritual by telling us something else: what Arkady is really perceiving in that moment. The parenthetical exclamation—"How shapely her figure seemed to him, engulfed in the grey shimmer of black silk."—is a glimpse into what that ritual of parting masks. The gaze of the young man is directed at the woman's figure (*stan*), paradoxically disrobed by allusion to the black silk that cloaks it. The dialogue that follows this narrated gaze will in turn be an "unmasking" of Arkady, who attempts to hide from Bazarov the real nature of his admiration for Odintseva. Bazarov's role as "unmasker" is here jovial, masculine, insinuating—but it is a frivolous rehearsal of more serious destruction. By disclosing Arkady's true sentiments Bazarov destroys the masks of civility—he effects a drawing room attack on that "civilization" he so ardently denounced in polemic with Pavel.

Arkady's glance at Odintseva is parenthetical and hidden: Bazarov approaches his friend and, in the spirit of male gossip, attempts to give expression to the hidden glance; the words he uses are elemental, implicitly dismissive of attempts to "dress up" what such a glance means.

Arkady's response to this comment, as to all that follows, is denial:

> —Some landowner just told me that this lady is—*oh ho ho!* Anyway, he seemed like a fool. But what do you think, is she, in fact—*oh ho ho!*?
> —I don't completely understand that designation—answered Arkady.
> —Well, well! What an innocent! (VIII, 268)

Arkady—feigning innocence—refuses to be drawn into Bazarov's discourse; he refuses to admit that his own admiration of Odintseva's figure is akin to Bazarov's *oh-ho-ho!*: he insists on a linguistic distinction that marks a barrier of civility. The conversation about Odintseva, however, is not merely a dialogue of chivalry and bravado; the entire exchange is an assault (on Bazarov's part) on a culture that dissembles, presenting elegant form as a mask for something "unseemly." Bazarov's response to Arkady is to insist on what is hidden, to insist that outer form dissolves to reveal something darker: his citation of a popular proverb ("Still waters . . . you know how it goes!") and his comparison of Odintseva to ice cream—what is cold and solid melts—both attack surface stability. The manner in which he delivers the proverb, ending in ellipses, attempts to implicate Arkady in his playful destructions: Arkady again refuses, professing not to understand. (This profession of incomprehension will be Odintseva's later defense as well, masking her attraction to Bazarov and her flirtation with him.)

The proverbial words that Bazarov omits, which Arkady refuses to acknowledge, are demonic: "Devils lurk in still waters [*V tikhom omute, cherty vodiatsia*]." In a conversation that plays throughout with what is said and left unspoken, with intention and dissimulation, these unspoken words have an unexpected resonance: the devils that popular wisdom ascribes to the still depths seem to lurk beneath *all* the dissembling masks of Bazarov and Arkady's exchange—within Odintseva, within Arkady himself. These two are the passage's dissemblers: it is Bazarov who liberates the unspoken by giving it indecorous names.

The men's dialogue ends with one final example of displacement: Arkady reproaches Bazarov "not quite for that which displeased him" (VIII, 268). The point here is not that Arkady is not being wholly honest or "sincere"—which of course he isn't. The more crucial aspect of the entire exchange is its representation of culture as a mask, as forms that cloak the "unspeakable"—Arkady's glance and Bazarov's devils. Arkady's glance disrobes Odintseva—he sees her body beneath grey silk—but he will not admit to it, just as he finally will reproach Bazarov on a matter of "principle," rather than say what really bothers him. Arkady refuses Bazarov's dismantling of civility and principle, in a small encounter that anticipates the young Kirsanov's ultimate allegiances. The very oppositions upon which Bazarov insists—stillness and frenzy, form and dissolution—will finally be irrelevant to Arkady, whose future promises pastoral harmony with Katya. Arkady will soon become "domesticated," a fate Bazarov will not choose. The rhetoric of Bazarov's convictions—as of his teasing—is absolute, and will not admit the gentler resolutions.

When Bazarov enters Odintseva's household he comes to a structure of civility and decorum, a structure he will attempt to penetrate and dissolve in the person of Odintseva. Her house—emblematic here of the woman—is a barricade thrown up against nature, lacking in the pastoral simplicity of either the Kirsanov or Bazarov households. When Katya enters Odintseva's drawing room with a dog and laden with flowers, the contrast with her elder sister is pointed. Katya is at home with a nature that is, for her, gentle; for Odintseva, the natural world is an object of indifference—but also of fear. "Katya *adored* nature, and Arkady loved it, although he didn't dare admit it; Odintseva was fairly indifferent to nature, as was Bazarov" (VIII, 286). Odintseva, as we later discover, will not frequent her garden portico after seeing a grass snake there (VIII, 374);

it is in this portico that Arkady proposes to Katya. That Odintseva fears, and shuns, an animal that is tame, is emblematic of her response to everything that lies beyond her manor walls. If the grass snake she fears seems almost too obviously phallic, it is well to remember that the snake is also the biblical emblem of sensuality, a sensuality with which Arkady and Katya—like all couples of pastoral innocence—seem to exist in happy equilibrium.

The encounters of Bazarov and Odintseva, however, depict neither pastoral nor equilibrium, but a play of sensuality which is tinged with predation. If pastoral represents a natural world that has been humanized (conventionalized), Bazarov and Odintseva allude, in their desire, to a human world made animalistic: they flirt with descent into the inhuman, the passional, the formless. The hunter, as conventional figure, is unknown to the traditions of pastoral, but it is hunting, predation, will—in all their etymological complexity—that haunt the scenes of Odintseva and Bazarov's encounter. ("Bazarov was a great lover of women [*velikii okhotnik do zhenshchin*]"; "[Odintseva] willingly [*okhotno*] remained alone with him and willingly conversed with him"; "I'm unhappy because I have neither the desire, nor the will to live [*okhoty zhit'*]"—VII, 286, 287, 292.) The hunter is unknown to pastoral because he does violence to the natural world, claims a supremacy of cunning and technique that destroys for him nature's benevolence; nature becomes his object, an object of will and desire, rather than a companion in his simplicity. He destroys that equilibrium of force that Turgenev described in "Journey into the Woodland" as nature's secret. The pastoral shepherd is liberated in his poverty from "the slavery of desire";[22] the hunter—and it is in this sense that Turgenev seems to choose his words—is in paradoxical bondage.

It is in the central encounters of Odintseva and Bazarov that Turgenev brings into most elemental contact this novel's opposites: unrestrained nature and a culture of dissimulation and restraint. Bazarov enters Odintseva's chambers as a figure possessed, whose passion has driven him to the solace of violent midnight walks ("He would set out for the woods and walk through them with great strides, breaking branches in his way and cursing under his breath both her and himself"—VIII, 287). Odintseva admits Bazarov "as though she wanted both to tempt him and to know herself" (VIII, 287). The deeper motivations for Odintseva's flirtation are nonetheless obscure, veiled— like so much else about this woman. The final unveiling that occurs in these encounters is of Odintseva to herself— a revelation startling in its suggestion of her kinship with Bazarov, a revelation from which she will flee to her familiar structures of order and repression.

The central gesture of these scenes is one of violent opening; it is stuffy, and Odintseva asks Bazarov to open the window: "Open that window—it feels a bit stuffy to me" (VIII, 290). When Bazarov does as she asks, the window flies with a crash: the warm, soft night air floods the room ("*temnaia miagkaia noch' glianula v komnatu*") (VII, 291). Odintseva tells Bazarov to lower the curtain—literally to cover with cloth the opening she has requested— and then embarks on a conversation with Bazarov that flirts with revelation. Their dialogue is interrupted by a description of the warm, sweet-smelling night that fills the room, of the "night freshness" that presses against the lowered curtain: "The lamp burned dimly in the darkened, fragrant, solitary room; through the occasionally swaying shades there flowed in the keen freshness of night, whose mysterious whispering was audible (VIII, 292). Throughout, Odintseva watches this veiled window—a window that stands as emblem of herself, of natural longing problematically hidden; the epithets of the room—fragrant (*blagovonnaia*), solitary (*uedinennaia*)—are also Odintseva's, echoing the earlier description of her emerging from the bath and the etymology of her own name. Odintseva watches this window as she will later watch her own face in the mirror—irresolute, apparently, unsure whether to welcome in her own person a similar gesture of opening and release. The woman who receives Bazarov is a study in nakedness and enclosure; as elsewhere, Turgenev's domestic details allude to a room's inhabitant. Like the narrative of Odintseva bathing and Arkady's glance, Turgenev's description disrobes the woman by alluding to what her clothes cover. "Odintseva threw her head back against the back of the chair and crossed her bare forearms on her breast. She seemed pale by the light of the single lamp, shaded in gauze of cutout paper. She was entirely covered in the soft folds of a full white dress; the very ends of her feet, also crossed, were barely visible" (VIII, 289).

Odintseva here flirts not only with Bazarov, but also with her own sensuality, a passional existence that her conventions so exquisitely cloak. She asks Bazarov to open the window—but it seems her real desire is that he open *her*, that he disrobe her (both literally and figuratively), that he forcefully cast off her chill restraint. When Bazarov leaves Odintseva on the first night, the narrator describes her as she sits in solitude: "Her plaited hair came unwound and fell like a dark snake on her shoulder" (VIII, 295). The dark serpent of Odintseva's hair is a figure for that sensuality she fears—the connection with the grass snake in the portico seems clear. What has happened here, though, is that the grass snake is no longer outside the manor—in a garden portico—but has come inside, has in fact become a part of Odintseva herself. Turgenev's intent is not, I think, purely conventional; he is not merely depicting another Cleopatra of the Steppes.[23] His introduction of motifs associated with a literary type serves his central problematic: the relationship of men and women to their own passional nature. Odintseva's fear of nature, of sexuality, will extend to Bazarov ("I'm afraid of that man"—VIII, 301); it is her fear that erects all the barriers of her life.

Odintseva's encounters with Bazarov bring what is most feared into most intimate proximity: not only Bazarov's embrace, but Odintseva's vision of her own face in the mirror, transform the domestic and familiar into something alien, unknown. The narrator's description of Odintseva after Bazarov's second evening visit closes with another revelation of her sensuality—only this time, Odintseva sees *herself*; it is not merely the narrator (and we) who see her: "(Or?)—she spoke suddenly, then stopped and shook back her hair. . . . She caught sight of herself in the mirror; her head, thrust back and with a mysterious smile on half-closed, half-opened eyes and lips, seemed to speak to her in that moment of something at which she herself grew confused" (VIII, 300). Odintseva has accomplished what she intended: she has come to know herself. Like all elemental knowledge—both biblical and Freudian—her knowledge is sexual. Odintseva's vision of herself is also a final commentary on her remark to Bazarov—"You know, you're the same as I am" (VIII, 292). The contextual motivation for that remark had to do with curiosity and the capacity for enthusiasm (*uvlekat'sia*); in Odintseva's final glance into the mirror, however, the identity is more elemental. Before looking into the mirror, she recalls Bazarov's "animal-like face" (*zverskoe litso*); it is that memory that precedes the vision of her *own* face—transformed into a face of brutal passion.

Odintseva's response to Bazarov's embrace is similar to Arkady's repulsion of his friend's masculine intimacies: she claims misunderstanding. "You didn't understand me. . . . I didn't understand you—and you didn't understand me" (VIII, 299). Rather than admit identity, the sudden collapse of barriers, Odintseva insists that communication failed—an insistence that is itself an exemplary "civil" resolution. Her disclaimers reerect the boundaries that had fallen, and trade customary dissimulation for darker revelations. Still, after Bazarov leaves, Odintseva hovers about the emblems of her self-revelation, emblems of what she has repressed: the window and the mirror. "She kept walking back and forth across her room . . . stopping occasionally, either in front of the window or the mirror" (VIII, 299). Emblems of flirtation with desire, they also mark the point Odintseva will not transgress: the point beyond which she sees "emptiness . . . or formlessness" (VIII, 300).

Odintseva withdraws from an encounter she obscurely desires, but fears; it is a retreat Turgenev clearly endorses—a retreat that may in fact stand as emblematic of his own narrative distance from Bazarov, an alien hero who he became intimate with, but expelled.[24] The characters of this novel to whom Turgenev stands closest are, in fact, those who enter most consciously into conflict with Bazarov: Pavel and Odintseva. It is these figures of order and elegant culture whose insight and distance are closest to the author's: for all the affection with which he draws Russia's pastoral figures, Turgenev's eye is alien, "superfluous" to that world, as is Pavel's in his visit to Fenichka's room. The authorial consciousness, that overarching mind that gives the narrative its form, is touched by a knowledge more bitter than that possessed by either Kirsanov or the elder Bazarov: the vision of "emptiness . . . or formlessness" beyond the barriers of decorum does not belong to them. It is this distinction that Bazarov articulates in his Pascalian nostalgia for simplicity: "They're there—my parents, that is—occupied and unconcerned at their own insignificance, there's no stink of nothingness for them . . . while I . . . I feel only boredom and malice" (VIII, 323).[25]

Turgenev ends his novel by returning us to the world of pastoral, to the figures of Baucis and Philemon from Ovid's *Metamorphoses*. When Bazarov's parents kneel at their son's graveside—in an enclosed plot where two trees stand—they evoke the harmonic resolution of the Latin poet, whose couple end their days as guardians of the temple, transformed finally into an oak and a linden: "An iron fence surrounds [the grave]; two young fir trees have been planted at each end: Evgeny Bazarov is buried in this grave" (VIII, 401).

Turgenev's novel ends by an evocation of transformation that draws on the Latin lyricist and the traditions of pastoral, a transformation that implies harmony, resolution, and endurance. Ovid's work, however, is as filled with stories of violent metamorphoses as it is with tales of the peaceful permutations of suffering: Turgenev's novel alludes to one of the *Metamorphoses'* more violent tales in its rendering of Bazarov's death. Bazarov's transgression of culture and his painful death echo Ovid's rendering of the story of Actaeon, a hero whose transformation images destruction rather than reward. Actaeon's death—he was devoured by his own hounds—will also be Bazarov's.

In the scene that describes Bazarov's death, Turgenev's hero falls into delirium, and is possessed by a vision of dogs; he describes this vision to his father:

Even now I'm not quite sure I'm expressing myself clearly. As I was lying here, it seemed to me that red dogs were running around me, and you were pointing over me, like you do over a black grouse.

And now it's back to my dogs once more. Strange! I want to keep my thoughts on death, and nothing comes of it. I see some kind of spot . . . and nothing more. (VIII, 390)

These passages—like the whole account of Bazarov's death—are startling in their elemental power; they are also puzzling: Turgenev uses the hero's delirium to represent his dying, in images that both arrest and confound the reader. Bazarov, in this passage, sees himself amidst red dogs: but in a position radically different from his earlier stature as hunter (*okhotnik*). If Bazarov's father stands above him, pointing, as a dog does in pursuit of prey, then Bazarov *is* the prey, and the dogs have come to devour him.

This passage is arresting not merely because Turgenev uses delirium in a manner similar to that in *On the Eve* (both "positive heroes," Insarov and Bazarov, succumb to a language that will not cohere to their much-vaunted realms, the political and the scientific). It strikes us further because it returns us to the language of metamorphosis in which Turgenev first conceived of his hero ("I dreamt of a gloomy figure, wild and large, grown half out of the soil"), and because it returns us to the concerns of pastoral, equilibrium, and destruction that are central to *Fathers and Children*.

The hunter who is hounded by his own dogs is, in classic mythology, Actaeon, whose death is willed by Diana after he has seen her in a forest bathing. Diana, chagrined that Actaeon has seen her naked, transforms the hunter into a stag, who is then devoured by his own dogs. Actaeon is destroyed for an involuntary transgression: to see Diana naked is, apparently, to enter a realm of taboo in which volition is irrelevant.[26]

The scene of Bazarov's death, and the allusion to Actaeon, return us to the central theme of the novel: Bazarov's encounter with Odintseva, his entry into her household, his passionate embrace. It is, of course, the narrator—and not Bazarov—who has seen Odintseva naked; Turgenev reallots the mythic roles, and makes his Actaeon a willful—not innocent—transgressor. Turgenev nonetheless retains the act of sexual violence that lies at the archaic center of the Ovidian story,[27] and makes that act emblematic of political transgressions. If Bazarov's throwing open of Odintseva's window is a metaphor for his desire to rape her, it is also a metaphor for his political desires: his longing to break into the kingdom of order, that paternal realm over which Odintseva presides. What Turgenev conflates, at his novel's center, are two acts of elemental transgression, acts of violence against body and *polis*: rape and revolution. It is symptomatic of Turgenev's aesthetic, both that he will veil those elemental acts, and that his narrative will work to reestablish the violated order. Turgenev's plot submits Bazarov to the forms of culture he has spurned—to those forms that contain eros and aggression: Bazarov's flirtation with Fenichka is a ritual of pastoral, filled with the *topoi* of sublimated eroticism;[28] his duel with Pavel sublimates violence in a highly conventionalized ritual.

Ovid veils, as does Turgenev, the act of rape to which

the Actaeon story alludes. The metamorphosis of Actaeon into a stag is, however, present in all versions of the story—a transformation that, if we interpret the tale as being about man's urge to violate woman, seems to be less the consequence of Diana's curse than of Actaeon's own desire. His desire is in itself brutal; the change of outer form follows an inner metamorphosis. That Turgenev retains the "psychology of metamorphosis,"[29] the notion of a regression from the human to the animal, is suggested in his description of Bazarov's embrace and Odintseva's response: Bazarov's face is "bestial," while Odintseva's own face is transformed by desire. Both Bazarov and Odintseva experience the metamorphosis of passion.

That passion is destructive is both a psychological and political truth for Turgenev: violation of the taboo—for both Actaeon and Bazarov—leads to their being literally consumed by the animal world. We will understand the importance of this novel's ending, and of the pastoral for Turgenev, only if we accept the essential identity of his sexual and social insights. Turgenev does indeed resolve his novel with a celebration of form and order—but an order that is open, not repressive. Turgenev's pastoral resolutions evoke the possibility of an existence that does not violate society's most fundamental boundaries: the epilogue's double weddings are comedy's convention for the restoration of order. What is restored in *Fathers and Children* is not, however, merely the past: Nikolay Kirsanov marries Fenichka (at Pavel's insistence)—the plebeian does after all enter the manor, but in an act that is legitimate, not transgressive.

Pavel's orchestration of the novel's ending is perhaps one final "wink" at a figure who stands so close to the author—for Turgenev's own consciousness is closest to Pavel's in his irrevocable knowledge of the "almost meaningless" that lurks both within and without the human form. The imagined social form of the novel's resolution is not, however, the structure associated with either Pavel or Odintseva. The gestural and social ideal of the novel will remain Arkady's: the throwing off of the heavy coat, the opening to his father and to nature, which was narrated at the novel's beginning. Turgenev imagines a world that can dispense with severe repression—both sexual and political—a world that is blessed by openness and equilibrium. The novel is representative of its time in perhaps just this sense: that such imagination was still possible. In 1909, writing at a moment beyond such possibility, the symbolist writer Dmitry Merezhkovsky turned with regret and chagrin to Turgenev, now eclipsed by writers of very different imaginations: "Didn't our revolution fail because there was too much in it of Russian extremity, too little of European measure; too much of L. Tolstoy and Dostoevsky, too little Turgenev."[30] What is manifest in *Fathers and Children* is Turgenev's knowledge of what lay immanent in Bazarov the revolutionary. Kukshina—Turgenev's parody of a nihilist—lives in a house that burns down every five years. Turgenev's novel makes here its own image of universal conflagration: Kukshina's fires, however, unlike Bazarov's dogs, will consume not the transgressor, but culture itself. Turgenev does not depict this conflagration— though he alludes to it—for the same reason that he does not depict the meaningless (*bessmyslie*) or the formless (*bezobrazie*): his novel is itself an icon of that culture he defends—restraint, order, form. Beyond that lies "emptiness": *nihil*.

CONCLUSION

THE NOVELS that form the center of this book were written in the brief period between the death of Nicholas the First and the emancipation of the serfs in 1861—a period during which educated Russians experienced a revival of hopes for the political and cultural future of their country. Turgenev's novels were written in the midst of that awakening and ferment, and were with justice read as being intimately concerned with the course Russia was taking, and might take. The great debates over these novels centered primarily on individual heroes and their truth to life, and elevated Turgenev's work of these years to a place of enormous social significance, as his novels became touchstones of principle and position. In the process, however, certain clichés about Turgenev and his novels were formed—clichés that have proved tenacious, and ultimately detrimental to the works themselves. I suggest this not necessarily because those readings are wrong, but because they have prevented later generations from reading Turgenev outside of certain foregone conclusions about his work: the terms of early debates—the superfluous man, the clash of love and duty, the emergence of the "new man"—have remained, confounded only by readings that acclaim Turgenev as the eulogist of the landed gentry, the singer of virginal love, the aging pessimist.

I have, by and large, dispensed with such assumptions about Turgenev—preferring, rather, to look to his texts to infer the character of the man who wrote them. The author emerges from this reading a figure more complex and modern than the traditional clichés allow. That is, no doubt, due in part to my own modernity; but Turgenev's novels challenge and compel because they are constructed of tensions still felt: between the intimate and the political, between desire and restraint, between fantasy and recognition. The work of reading and criticism involves finding words for an experience that is at once elemental and complex: my readings are attempts to articulate that experience, to argue that Turgenev is the property not only of the past, but of the present.

My tendency has been to resist generalization—for it is precisely such generalities that have relegated Turgenev to mediocrity—but general senses of Turgenev's craft and commitment do surface from these essays in close reading.

As a social novelist, Turgenev returns repeatedly to lyric as a point of solitude beyond the social. In his contemplations of nature, as in his inference of human enigma, the narrative persona who shapes Turgenev's novels is a lyricist manqué, who sees the human drama within the context of nature's cycles, her epochal unconcern with the intimate tragedies of men and women. Nature gives to Turgenev both his language and his concerns; the possibility of a life in society that is "natural" but also just.

Turgenev's uses of the pastoral are various, and connected to his concern with the relationship of society and the natural world: in Lavretsky's Slavophile idyll at Vasilevskoe, and in the depiction of the "fathers" as representative of continuity and measure. Turgenev's gravitation toward the genre comes as no surprise, for a major focus of his writings is Russia's break with the traditions of her countryside. His polemic with Slavophile pastoral is succeeded by an epilogue that casts the future as an idyll of liberation; *Fathers and Children* envisions the triumphs of continuity and agronomy over radical change. Turgenev thus both polemicizes with, and embraces to his own ends, the pastoral. His use of pastoral in *Fathers and Children* is not motivated, however, by the desire to escape history—a motive he attributes in *A Nest of Gentry* to the Slavophiles—but by his fear of revolution, of the unleashing of destructive psychological and political forces. Both *A Nest of Gentry* and *Fathers and Children* counsel recognition of reality, the enduring pressure of past events. In *A Nest of Gentry*, however, the past is ominous; in *Fathers and*

Children, past is present as tradition—a tradition of devotion and work that Turgenev opposes to Bazarov's revolutionary intentions. If Turgenev's uses of the pastoral appear contradictory—a possibility I have suggested in my discussion of the epilogue of *A Nest of Gentry*—this is no doubt because his own deep love for Russia was marked by a painful sense of the violence and darkness of her history. The Catullan mixture of love and hate that is characteristic of Potugin in *Smoke* ("I passionately love and passionately hate Russia"—IX, 173) is, after all, Turgenev's.

Turgenev's sense of measure, of the limits and possibilities of historical change, his perception of the gulfs of passion and blindness that overtake the most well-intentioned men and women—all derive from the compassionate observation of both intimate and historical existence. His novels imply the historical not only in their topicality—in the accurate representation of generational style and cultural polemic—but also in their suggestion that the forces that shape human lives shape history, as well: the counterpoint of enclosure and enlightenment in *A Nest of Gentry*, of will and contemplation in *On the Eve*, of destruction and restraint in *Fathers and Children*, structure both intimate and historical plot in these novels. Turgenev's counsels of restraint, as I have suggested in my reading of *Fathers and Children*, extend from his aesthetics to his political psychology: only in recognition of the negative—of enclosure, of passion, of inertia—will men and women be able to embrace the positive.

What strikes us about Turgenev's novels is his ability to link the historical and the intimate, the aesthetic and the political, the impulses of our reading with those of his writing—in ways that are, I believe, divergent from the clichés of nineteenth-century criticism. Turgenev engages us in a beautiful illusion—of Russia as mother earth, nurturer of her prodigal sons—only to dash that illusion. His strategy allies us with Lavretsky, but it also reminds us of the enchantments that *On the Eve* implies: the worlds we inhabit in reading Turgenev are, like the space beneath the lime tree, timeless and free—as no space in either nature or history is. The enormous faith that Turgenev invested in the Russian language—as guarantor of a future liberation, of the realization of justice and freedom—was balanced by his anxious recognition of the futility of art's consolations: "I mould my speech in roundness, take comfort in the sound and harmony of words. Thus, like a sculptor, like a master goldsmith, I diligently fashion and engrave and make variously beautiful that chalice in which I will offer poison to myself" (XIII, 205). The evidence of both nature and history sobers Turgenev, who finds little promise of heroic fulfillment or intimate happiness. The men and women in his novels who are happy and fulfilled, are those whose ambitions are most modest, whose projects extend, but remain fundamentally within, the traditions of the past and the balances of nature.

In his fourth, and perhaps most "modern" novel, Turgenev brings to fullness his meditations on the relationship of men and women to nature—to a nature that is their own, yet alien. The recognition of limitations—of reality perceived as fundamentally limiting—and reconciliation with that reality is fundamental, the novel implies, not merely to civilization, but to survival. *Fathers and Children*, I have suggested, is itself an icon of those values it embraces: order, restraint, cultural tradition. The same might be argued of all of Turgenev's mature work, that seeks to reconcile, without illusions, the exigencies of reality with a vision of human possibility. "I am not sure that the method of Turgenev—this perfect proportion, this vigilant but never theoretic intelligence, this austere art of omission—is not that which in the end proves most satisfying to the civilized mind."[1] What T. S. Eliot here implies is that Turgenev's aesthetic restraint must be seen as bound to his moral and political convictions: that his art and intelligence are indissoluble. In reading Turgenev, I have undertaken to understand form—the infinite, urgent choices of the artist—as they embody the deepest convictions of the form-giving spirit. Turgenev's matter may be given, but his creation is free.

NOTES

INTRODUCTION

1. I. S. Turgenev, *Polnoe sobranie sochinenii i pisem v dvadtsati vos'mi tomakh*, 12 (Moscow, 1960–68), p. 303. All citations from Turgenev's works and letters are drawn from this edition, and will henceforth be noted in the text. The letter P denotes *Pis'ma*.

2. Helen Muchnic demonstrates this situation in first claiming Turgenev's work as a "resume of social conditions and intellectual controversies in Russia from the forties to the seventies," and then questioning whether the work offers "insight into the broadly human as well as into the problems of the nation, whether it is as deep as it is clear." *An Introduction to Russian Literature* (New York, 1964), pp. 103–4.

3. Mikhail Gershenzon, *Mechta i mysl' I. S. Turgeneva* (Providence, R.I., 1970), p. 67.

4. The extremely interesting study by Marina Ledkovsky, *The Other Turgenev: From Romanticism to Symbolism* (Wurzburg, 1973) is nonetheless marred by this premise: that Turgenev is "universal" in his stories and "dated" in his novels.

5. ". . . the artist has nothing to say about the process of creation, he is left only to point us toward his work; and indeed, only there will we seek him." M. M. Bakhtin, "Avtor i geroi v èsteticheskoi deiatel'nosti," in *Èstetika slovesnogo tvorchestva* (Moscow, 1986), p. 11.

6. For a discussion of Turgenev criticism that is attentive to the shaping of such criticism by cultural climate, see Robert L. Jackson, "The Turgenev Question," *Sewanee Review* 93 (1985), pp. 300–309.

7. I am indebted here to John Ellis, who suggests that literary works may be defined as such not by virtue of any intrinsic characteristics, but in the manner by which they are treated by a given community. I am then defining as literary those texts that survive when liberated from their original situation. John M. Ellis, *The Theory of Literary Criticism: A Logical Analysis* (Berkeley, 1974).

144

8. *The Letters of William James*, vol. 1, edited by Henry James (Boston, 1920), p. 185.

9. I quote here Frank Kermode, *The Genesis of Secrecy: On the Interpretation of Narrative* (Cambridge, Mass. 1979), p. 45.

CHAPTER ONE, "RHETORIC AND SINCERITY"

1. "The very type of Turgenev's novels is linked with George Sand. G. Sand wrote, in opposition to Balzac, personal novels ('novels of the hero' [*roman o geroe*]), novels of culture." L. V. Pumpianskii, "Turgenev i zapad," in *I. S. Turgenev: Materialy i issledovaniia*, ed. N. L. Brodskii (Orel, 1940), p. 92.

2. For a history of the reception of the play, see PSS III, pp. 403–27.

3. M. O. Gabel' deals extensively with the literary and historical prototypes of Rudin: "Tvorcheskaia istoriia romana *Rudin*," *Literaturnoe nasledstvo* 76 (Leningrad, 1967), pp. 9–70. N. L. Brodskii, in his article "Bakunin i Rudin," suggests that the contrast between the Rudin of the first and second parts of the novel corresponds to Bakunin's transition from "right" to "left" Hegelianism. *Katorga i ssylka*, no. 5 (Moscow, 1926).

4. Fet, in his memoir of Turgenev, quotes the novelist's amazement at his youthful philosophical facility: "Several days ago I looked over my notes on philosophy from Berlin. Good God! Is it possible that I once wrote that and put it all together? Let them kill me if I'm capable of understanding even one word of it." *I. S. Turgenev v vospominaniiakh sovremennikov* (1:196). The Soviet scholar A. I. Batiuto discusses at length Turgenev's criticism of philosophical systems, but is also sensitive to Turgenev's lifelong philosophical interests and erudition. *Turgenev—romanist* (Leningrad, 1972), pp. 46–159.

5. A. I. Batiuto discusses the instability of Turgenev's own use of generic terms in referring to his longer prose works: see "Problematika zhanra v romanistike Turgeneva," in *Turgenev—romanist*.

6. S. Orlovskii points out, in an early study of Turgenev's lyric verse, that while the author vigorously condemned his early poetry, Turgenev himself "permeates" his stories with his verse, itself the "source of his creative work." *Lirika molodogo Turgeneva* (Prague, 1926), pp. 12–20.

7. As Richard Freeborne puts it, "All Turgenev's heroes em-

body ideas and aspire to emulate ideals." *Turgenev: The Novelist's Novelist* (London, 1960), p. 75.

8. W. Lednicki, "*The Nest of Gentlefolk* and the 'Poetry of Marriage and the Hearth,' " in *Bits of Table Talk on Pushkin, Mickiewicz, Goethe, Turgenev and Sienkiewicz* (The Hague, 1956), p. 65. The Soviet scholar I. Al'mi is similarly disdainful of Turgenev's endings, calling them "compromises" with "the average." "Pushkinskaia traditsiia v romane Turgeneva *Ottsy i deti*," *Pushkinskii sbornik* (Pskov, 1973), p. 125.

9. Almost all of the memoirs of the period offer anecdotes of hyperverbosity and personal failure. See P. Miliukov, "Liubov' u idealistov tridtsatykh godov," in *Iz istorii russkoi intelligentsii* (St. Petersburg, 1903).

10. "There's not a minute I've lived without consciousness" (*U menia net minuty, prozhitoi bez soznaniia*). Quoted in Brodskii, "Bakunin i Rudin," p. 152.

11. Hegelian terminology arguably gives Rudin his name: ". . . the consciousness of being the instrument [*soznanie byt' orudiem*] of these higher powers should replace for man all other joys" (VI, 270). In *A Nest of Gentry* Mikhalevich, Lavretsky's friend from earlier, Idealist days, repeats this tag, and then remembers he doesn't believe it any more: ". . . there I was the instrument of fate [*ia byl tut orudiem* sud'by]—wait a minute, what am I lying for,—there's no fate involved; it's an old habit of expressing myself inexactly" (VII, 202).

12. —The bear wanted to get to water. . .
—Is that the mark [*sled*] of his paw?—I asked?
—His: but the water's dried up. There's his mark on that pine as well. (VII, 59)
The narrator and his peasant guide later see the "marks" of their hunting companion: "We came out, but didn't find Kondrat for a while. . . . Only the marks [*sledy*] of his movement were evident on separately standing trees" (VII, 61).

13. On the association of metonymy with prose, see Roman Jakobson, "Two Aspects of Language and Two Types of Aphasic Disturbances," in *Fundamentals of Language* (The Hague, 1971), pp. 69–96.

14. Panaev's *Rodstvenniki* is closest in plot to *Rudin*: Grigor'ev's "Moe znakomstvo s Vitalinym" (1845) expresses a revulsion with words, and a longing for "a man with whom you can now and then be silent"—both evidenced in *Rudin*. *Repertuar i panteon*

(1845) 11:8, p. 512. Cf. N. L. Brodskii, "Genealogiia romana *Rudin*," in *Pamiati P. N. Sakulina* (Moscow, 1931), pp. 24–25.

15. For a reading of the novel's concern with language and truth, see my essay, "The Death of Rhetoric in *Rudin*," in *Russian Literature* 16 (1984), pp. 375–84.

16. In this view, Lezhnev's praise of Rudin in chapter 12 is an emendation on Turgenev's part, motivated by a reappraisal of the generation of idealists on the historian Granovsky's death. Cf. PSS VI, 556, and M. O. Gabel', "Tvorcheskaia istoriia. . . ."

17. S. Orlovskii, in her study of Turgenev's lyric poetry, discusses what Turgenev himself—in another letter to Tolstaya—recognized as his "duality": "What you say about the double man in me is completely just, only perhaps you don't know the reasons for that doubleness" (P, III, 65). Orlovskii cites various memoirs to document the radically different impressions Turgenev made in society and among intimate friends: "Lack of constraint and open simplicity alternated in him with modish posing and insincerity, as soon as he found himself among the literary groups of the capitals." *Lirika molodogo Turgeneva* (Prague, 1926), p. 57. The facility with which Turgenev's narrators adopt the tones of high society is no doubt a legacy of Turgenev's own youth.

18. Turgenev here retains the ambiguity and resonance of Griboedov, whose play "Woe from Wit" is so frequently echoed in *Rudin*.

19. For a brief discussion of the terms of this debate, see Peter Brooks, *The Melodramatic Imagination* (New York, 1985), chapter 3: "The Text of Muteness."

20. This story's concern with muteness and emotion was made apparent to me only in a different medium: the powerful dramatization of "Mumu" by the Malyi Dramaticheskii Teatr (*Small Dramatic Theatre*) in Leningrad, a production I saw during the winter of 1985.

21. Tolstoy is quoted by N. L. Brodskii in "Khudozhniki slova o Turgeneve," in *Turgenev i ego vremeni* (Moscow-Petrograd, 1923), p. 6.

CHAPTER TWO, "GOSSIP, SILENCE, STORY"

1. Several critics have given attention to the symbolic significance of Turgenev's use of domestic space, though none have

treated it as closely as one might wish. The relationship of house to garden is, for example, the topic of an essay by N. Ingham, "Turgenev in the Garden," *Mnemozina*, 1974. One of the best essays on *A Nest of Gentry*, and one that has been enormously suggestive for my own work, is W. Lednicki's *"The Nest of Gentlefolk* and the 'Poetry of Marriage and the Hearth,' " in his *Bits of Table Talk on Pushkin* . . . (The Hague, 1956). Lednicki mentions, though he does not develop, the novel's spatial allegory when he speaks of its "division of life into a superior and an inferior zone" (p. 80).

2. Treatments of the dramatic affinities of Turgenev's narratives generally address their use of dialogue. See V. Baevskii, "Rudin I. S. Turgeneva (k voprosu o zhanre)," *Voprosy literatury*, no. 2 (1958); and L. Hellgren, *Dialogue in Turgenev's Novels: Speech Introductory Devices* (Stockholm, 1980). For a discussion of the indebtedness of Turgenev's novels to the drama in terms of their scenic organization, see V. M. Markovich, *I. S. Turgenev i russkii realisticheskii roman* (Leningrad, 1982), pp. 134–39. Markovich's discussion of the adherence of *A Nest of Gentry* to classical models of tragedy is particularly illuminating.

3. Alexander Herzen's famous description of Hegelian language opposes abstraction and simplicity: "Our young philosophers spoiled not merely their language but their understanding; their attitude toward life and reality became scholastic—that academic understanding of simple things that Goethe made such brilliant fun of in his dialogue of Mephistopheles and the student." *Byloe i dumy*, pt. 4, ch. 25, in A. I. Gertsen, *Sobranie sochinenii v vos'mi tomakh*, vol. 5 (Moscow, 1975), p. 101.

4. Of *War and Peace*, Turgenev wrote: "And as far as the so-called psychology of Tolstoy goes, I could say a great deal: there is no true evolution in a single character . . . but there is the old trick of rendering the hesitations and vibrations of one and the same emotion, situation, which he mercilessly puts into the mouth and consciousness of each of his heroes: I—well—love, but in reality I hate, etc., etc." Turgenev's intention in his own prose was to have the "psychologist cede to the artist"—as he put it in his review of Ostrovsky's *The Poor Bride* (V, 391).

5. B. Eikhenbaum, *Lev Tolstoi*, vol. 1 (Leningrad, 1928–31), p. 345. Eikhenbaum refers to a genre whose practitioners included Marlinsky, Panaev, Odoevsky, and Rostopchina.

6. On the society tale in Russian literature of the early nine-

teenth century, see R. V. Iezuitova, "Svetskaia povest,' " in B. S. Meilakh, editor, *Russkaia povest' XIX v.* (Leningrad, 1973), pp. 169–99; and Elizabeth C. Shepard, "The Society Tale and the Innovative Argument in Russian Prose Fiction of the 1830's," *Russian Literature* vol. 10 (1981), pp. 111–61.

7. In his essay on the novels of Evgeniya Tur, Turgenev notes the existence of Dumas-style novels in Russia, but asks the reader to ignore them as a narrative model (V, 373). The editors of the Academy edition assume Turgenev shared Belinsky's view of Dumas: "Many people start a Dumas novel as they would a fairy tale, knowing ahead what it's about; they read it in order to be diverted by unheard of adventures while they're reading, and then they forget them forever" (V, 634).

8. Here Turgenev's narrator adopts the same tone as his characters, descending for a moment to their "worldly" perspective. The switch is, of course, ironic.

9. The entire opening passage of the story, with its emphasis on silence and alienation, is reminiscent of Pascal's words, "The eternal silence of these infinite spaces frightens me." *Pensées* (New York, 1941), pp. 74–75.

10. For a discussion of this passage and its significance for Turgenev's aesthetics, see Robert L. Jackson, "The Root and the Flower. Dostoevsky and Turgenev: A Comparative Esthetic," *Yale Review* (Winter 1974), pp. 228–50.

11. Orthodox spirituality is grounded in the apopathic tradition, which asserts the impossibility of positive statements about God. See B. Krivocheine, *The Ascetic and Theological Teaching of Gregory Palamas* (London, 1954).

12. Elizabeth C. Shepard briefly discusses the role of gossip in society tales; see "The Society Tale and the Innovative Argument . . . ," p. 135.

13. Patricia Meyer Spacks, *Gossip* (New York, 1985). Spacks looks at gossip in relation to narrative; her work views gossip as meaningful "idle talk" potentially subversive of public discourse.

CHAPTER THREE, "HISTORY AND IDYLL IN *A NEST OF GENTRY*"

1. See VII, pp. 305 and 451. The edition of Danilov that Turgenev read was *Drevnie rossiiskie stikhotvoreniia sob. Kirsheiu Danilovym* (Moscow, 1818).

2. Anton's comments on Glafira's death—"Every man . . . is

doomed to devour himself" (VII, 244) echo the words of Ecclesiastes: "The fool folds his hands, and eats his own flesh." *Ecclesiastes* 4:5.

3. The novel on which Turgenev was working was entitled *Two Generations* (*Dva pokoleniia*); he was never satisfied with the manuscript, and destroyed it.

4. On the genesis of *A Nest of Gentry*, see VI, 457.

5. One might also mention Tolstoy's "Morning of a Landowner," another work published in 1856 that narrates the encounter of Europeanized good intentions and peasant wisdom.

6. Wayne Booth argues this point in his classic work, *The Rhetoric of Fiction* (Chicago, 1961)—arguing it against adherents of Henry James and his canonization of narrative "showing."

7. V. M. Markovich points to the naming of Lavretsky after a martyr, suggesting quite correctly that "details of this sort are usually significant in Turgenev." *I. S. Turgenev i russkii realisticheskii roman XIX veka* (Leningrad, 1982), p. 165.

8. The *Stradanie* of Theodore Stratilatus is recounted on February 8th in the liturgical cycle. The work might have been known to Turgenev in several ways: as read during services; in the *Chet'ye minei* of Dmitrii Rostovskii; or in the shorter edition of selected *Lives* published by Bakhmetov, *Izbrannye zhitiia sviatykh, kratko izlozhennye* (Moscow, 1858). Turgenev's familiarity with and creative use of Russian hagiographic sources has been argued by N. F. Droblenkova, " 'Zhivye Moshchi' Turgeneva," in *Turgenevskii sbornik*, 5 (Leningrad, 1969), pp. 289–302.

9. "Common to Jews and Christians is the notion that the man who remains faithful to God in suffering, even to death, will receive from God his recompense. . .

"Similarly, in both traditions, faith which is unshakeable despite death gives to the martyr firm hope in immortality and the resurrection." *Dictionnaire de Spiritualité*, vol. 5, p. 726.

10. For a brilliant reading of *The Idiot* in this light, see M. J. Holquist, "The Gaps in Christology: The Idiot," in *Dostoevsky and the Novel* (Evanston, Ill., 1977), pp. 102–23.

11. The book to which Turgenev refers here, *Emvlemy i symvoly izbrannye* . . . (St. Petersburg, 1788), was enormously important to him in his own boyhood. See Anthony R. Hippisley, "The Emblem in Russian Literature," *Russian Literature* 16 (1984), pp. 289–304.

12. Critics frequently read Lavretsky's peasant lineage as a

positive attribute; Turgenev, however, associates the *muzhik* in Lavretsky with violence—here, with his desire physically to attack Varvara.

13. In his discussion of Turgenev's use of the Emblem book, Anthony Hippisley notes that "[Turgenev] has chosen emblems that were particularly enigmatic." See "The Emblem in Russian Literature," p. 289.

14. Quoted in E. Chmielewski, *Tribune of the Slavophiles* (University of Florida Press, 1962), pp. 35–36.

15. John 11. The Lazarus story is, of course, also central to *Crime and Punishment*, Dostoevsky's narrative of transgression and rebirth. The narrative of rebirth, however, is placed in Dostoevsky's novel in a crucially different relationship to narrated "history." Alexander Herzen uses the figures of Martha and Mary in a more "secular" context to refer to the pragmatist and visionary, respectively. See his "Endings and Beginnings" [*"Kontsy i nachala"*] of 1862.

16. Iurii Lotman describes the typology of rebirth as follows: "Temporary death, as a form of transition from one state to another—higher—is encountered in an extremely broad range of texts and rituals." "Proiskhozhdenie siuzheta v tipologicheskom osveshchenii," *Stat'i po tipologii kultury* (Tartu, 1970). In this study of linear and circular plot structures, Lotman notes Mikhalevich's verses in *A Nest of Gentry*, but does not examine the broader significance of rebirth motifs in the novel.

17. "We . . . discussed the original ritual of baptism, especially the curious archaic conception of it as an initiation connected with real peril of death. Such initiations were often connected with the peril of death and so served to express the archetypal idea of death and rebirth. Baptism had originally been a real submersion which at least suggested the danger of drowning." C. G. Jung, *Memories, Dreams, Reflections* (New York, 1965).

18. I take these terms from Frank Kermode's study of temporality in the novel, *The Sense of an Ending: Studies in the Theory of Fiction* (London, 1966). Kermode himself takes the terms from modern theology: "It is important that these modern theologians *want* these words to mean involved distinctions of the sort I have discussed . . . we need, for our obscure cultural ends, to observe distinctions between mere chronicity and times which are concordant and full," pp. 49–50.

19. This brief, allusive passage begs comparison with Tolstoy's

The Death of Ivan Ilych—where the ephemerality of the hero's life is made radically apparent in the presence of death.

20. "And then who says that man is destined to be free? History proves the opposite."

21. "Man is not born to be free." Turgenev here quotes Goethe's *Torquatto Tasso*, Act II, scene 1.

22. See, for instance, Henri Granjard, *Ivan Tourguénev et les courants politiques et sociaux de son temps* (Paris, 1966), pp. 273, 282.

23. For G. Bialyi, the "radiant poetry of the ending of *A Nest of Gentry* and Lavretsky's submission to the future generation constitute a triumph over the novel's 'pessimism.' " *Turgenev i russkii realizm* (Moscow-Leningrad, 1962), p. 110. Richard Freeborne attributes to Turgenev a balancing of pessimism in the individual and optimism in the ideological (*Turgenev: The Novelist's Novelist* [London, 1960], p. 115). As will become more fully apparent in my discussion of *Fathers and Children*, I think such an absolute separation of the personal and the ideological overstates the case.

24. Dostoevsky's comments on *A Nest of Gentry* were published in his *Diary of a Writer* for 1876, in an essay called "On Love for the People" (*"O liubvi k narodu"*). F. M. *Dostoevskii ob iskusstve* (Moscow, 1973), pp. 455–56.

25. Franco Venturi sums up Dobrolyubov's famous essay in these words in *Roots of Revolution* (Chicago, 1960), p. 192.

CHAPTER FOUR, *"ON THE EVE AND THE SIRENS OF STASIS"*

1. "As for the ancients, one of these days I plan to go to one of the islands with the *Odyssey* and stay there indefinitely."

2. Conservative critics attacked Elena for her unchaperoned meetings with Insarov, and her evident (though inexplicit) sexual surrender to him prior to marriage—both "revolutionary" breaks with decorum. Typical of the hysteria of such criticism is the review in *Domashniaia beseda* of 1860: "[Such heroines] are almost always discarded like a squeezed up lemon; then, having broken all connections with their families, with no honest means for their living, they go from hand to hand, until. . . . It's terrible to say how such heroines end up."

3. Henri Granjard suggests that *On the Eve* was born "of the enthusiasm and hopes that then filled Turgenev's heart and soul, looking forward at this time of his life, like the two heroes of the

novel, toward the horizon where the new dawn would glow."
Ivan Tourguénev et les courants . . . , p. 282. For G. Bialyi, as for
Dobrolyubov, the novel is essentially the portrait of the "new
people"—"consciously heroic natures"—who were to liberate
Russia. *Turgenev i russkii realizm*, p. 114.

4. The finest recent treatment of Turgenev in this light is Dale
Peterson's, in *The Clement Vision: Poetic Realism in Turgenev and
James* (Port Washington, N.Y., 1975).

5. S. Shatalov notes the presence of scenes reminiscent of
prose poems in works throughout Turgenev's career, and suggests that Turgenev knew of the genre from the time of his ear-
liest work in prose. *Problemy poetiki I. S. Turgeneva*, pp. 146–47.

6. For a history of the writing of *On the Eve*, see PSS VIII, pp.
496–509.

7. I am indebted here to Peter Brooks's analysis of ambition as
"not only a typical novelistic theme, but also a dominant dynamic of plot." *Reading for the Plot* (New York, 1984), p. 39.
Brooks is speaking primarily of Balzac and Dickens, novelistic
worlds in which the hero's private ambition is central—something very uncharacteristic of Russian nineteenth-century literature. It nonetheless seems to me that social/utopian ambition in
On the Eve shares the same "double" function as Brooks ascribes
to private ambition in other European novelists.

8. On Turgenev's fondness for, and literary use of Virgil from
The Huntsman's Sketches to *Spring Torrents*, see A. N. Egunov,
" 'Veshnie vody.' Latinskie ssylki v povesti Turgeneva," in *Tur-
genevskii sbornik*, 4, pp. 182–89.

9. As Circe warns Odysseus: "First you will come to the sirens
who enchant all who come near them. If anyone unwarily draws
in too close and hears the singing of the sirens, his wife and children will never welcome him home again, for they sit in a green
field and warble him to death with the sweetness of their song."
Odysseus, bk. XII, Trans. Samuel Butler (Chicago, 1952), p. 250.

10. See Joanna Hubbs, "The Worship of Mother Earth in Russian Culture," in *Mother Worship*, ed. J. P. Preston (Chapel Hill,
1982), p. 139.

11. As Shubin puts it: "Look at the river: it's as though it's
tempting us. The ancient Greeks would have seen a nymph. But
we're not Greeks, dear nymph! We're thick-skinned Scythians"
(VIII, 16). Shubin's banter is a good example of the way Turgenev

preserves a consciousness of antique models while at the same time marking ironic distance from them.

12. ". . . gentle, dreamy, lazy and a gourmand, fed on readings of Lamartine, at once insinuating and disdainful."

13. "What I took for courage in him, wasn't it merely the impertinence of a joker who knows one's kidding and makes you pay for your trouble? Oh! Illusions! There's how you're lost. . . . Mr. Lamartine, come sing that for me."

14. "Oh lake! the year has barely finished its course, and look! beside the cherished waves that she should have seen again I come to sit, on this rock where you saw her sit.

"One evening, do you remember? we floated in silence; on the water and beneath the skies we heard only, from afar, the noise of oarsmen who rhythmically struck the harmonious waves." Citations from Lamartine's poem are from *Oeuvres poétiques complètes de Lamartine* (Paris, 1963), pp. 38–40.

15. "Oh time! suspend your flight; and you, propitious hours! suspend your stream: Let us savor the rapid delights of the most beautiful of our days!

"There are enough unfortunates here who implore you, move on, move on for them; Take with their days the cares that consume them, Forget those who are happy.

"But in vain I plead for a few more moments, Time escapes me and flies; I say to this night: linger; and dawn comes to dispense the night.

"Then let us love, let us love! Let us make haste, and take our pleasure! Man has no harbor, time has no shore; it flows, and we pass on."

16. "Jealous time, is it possible that these drunken moments, when love pours happiness in long waves, will fly from us with the same speed as do days of unhappiness?"

17. "Eternity, nothingness, time past, deep abysses—what do you do with the days you swallow up?"

18. "Suddenly, accents unknown to the earth echoed from the charmed shore; the wave was attentive, and the voice that is dear to me let fall these words . . ."

19. The first italics here are mine; the second are Turgenev's.

20. Richard Gustafson, in his book on Afanasy Fet, points out the similarity between this passage from *On the Eve* and the poet's 1854 lyric, "Kak zdes' svezho pod lipoiu gustoiu . . ."; Gustafson suggests not influence but a case of "striving for the

same effect: the realization of a sensation by means of images."
The Imagination of Spring: The Poetry of Afanasy Fet (New Haven,
1966), pp. 133–35. Several Soviet scholars have suggested a broad
congruity between Fet and Turgenev: L. M. Lotman points to
parallels between several Fet poems and passages in "Asya"
("Turgenev i Fet," pp. 38–40), and V. M. Markovich has suggested a "Fet tonality" in much of Turgenev's lyricism, a longing
on the part of both artists to "hold the moment" in poetic representation. V. M. Markovich, *I. S. Turgenev i russkii realisticheskii
roman*, p. 160.

21. It is worth noting that the final analogue for Turgenev's
hero is Violetta; Insarov passes from heroic stature to a mortality
shared by courtesans.

22. Tony Tanner, in *Adultery in the Novel*, speaks of an "intimate alliance between the sea and illicit passion" throughout the
nineteenth-century novelistic tradition, p. 32. Turgenev uses the
image of a placid sea that masks turbulence and destruction as
an overture to his novel of passion and betrayal, *Spring Torrents*.

23. Turgenev worked with the poet Fet on the latter's translation of *Julius Caesar* during August of 1858, at Spasskoe, Turgenev's estate. The translation was published in *Biblioteka dlia chten-
iia*, no. 3 (1858).

24. S. Shatalov suggests that in works written after *Fathers and
Children*, Turgenev breaks with "rationalist" illumination of the
human psyche and adopts forms of interior speech. *Khudozhestvennyi mir I. S. Turgeneva* (Moscow, 1979), p. 215. Insarov's raving
suggests an earlier occurrence of this narrative technique.

25. The magistrate takes snuff from a box with "full-breasted"
nymphs on its lid: the reminiscence of classical grace in a seamy
setting is but one more allusion to the fall of the heroic.

26. Carolyn Heilbrun has suggested that "the birth of the
woman as hero occurred, insofar as one may date such an event,
in 1880, when almost at the same moment Ibsen and James in-
vented her." *Toward a Recognition of Androgyny*, p. 49. One might
suggest a more eastern birth, in the year 1859—a birth of which
Henry James was certainly aware. James said of *On the Eve*
(which he read in the French translation, *Hélène*): "The story is
all in the portrait of the heroine, who is a heroine in the literal
sense of the word; a young girl of a will so calmly ardent and
intense that she needs nothing but opportunity to become one of

the figures about whom admiring legend clusters." *Literary Criticism*, vol. 2, p. 978.

27. Turgenev's use of Pascalian language to articulate Bazarov's thoughts on the insignificance of human life has been noted by A. I. Batiuto, *Turgenev-romanist*, p. 62.

28. "What! can't we at least hold on to the trace [of our loves]? What? vanished for ever? What! completely lost?"

29. I am referring here to *Macbeth* (V, v), which Turgenev seems to echo in his reference to the end of the "petty game of life": ". . . Out, out, brief candle!/Life's but a walking shadow, a poor player/That struts and frets his hour upon the stage/And then is heard no more. It is a tale/Told by an idiot, full of sound and fury,/Signifying nothing."

30. "Zhenskie tipy v romanakh i povestiakh Pisemskogo, Turgeneva i Goncharova," in D. Pisarev, *Literaturnaia kritika v trekh tomakh*, vol. l, p. 227.

31. Virgil's *Aeneid*, translated by Robert Fitzgerald, p. 118.

CHAPTER FIVE, "THE DISMANTLING OF CULTURE"

1. Dmitrii Merezhkovskii, "Turgenev," in his *Polnoe sobranie sochinenii* vol. 17 (Moscow, 1914), p. 48.

2. One of the standard questions of criticism of the novel has to do with Bazarov as typical of the *raznochintsy*, or nongentry intelligentsia; there has been disagreement on this issue ever since Pisarev's seminal article and the furor that accompanied the novel's publication. E. Vodovozova, in her memoirs, gives a vivid description of a heated discussion of the justice—or injustice—of Turgenev's portrayal of the young radicals. See *Turgenev v vospominaniiakh sovremennikov* vol.1 (Moscow, 1983), pp. 345–50.

3. As will, I hope, be apparent from this essay, I am using the word "culture" in its broader sense—not merely in reference to art, literature, and music, but also as descriptive of that ensemble of gestures, conventions, and languages that constitute the humanly created.

4. William Empson, writing of Grey's "Elegy in a Country Churchyard," notes "By comparing the social arrangement to Nature he makes it seem inevitable, which it was not, and gives it a dignity which was undeserved." Empson, *Some Versions of Pastoral* (New York, 1974), p. 4.

5. For an excellent reading of this story's centrality to Turgenev's aesthetics, see Robert L. Jackson, "The Root and the Flower. Dostoevsky and Turgenev: A Comparative Esthetic," *Yale Review* (Winter 1974), pp. 228–50.

6. A. Walicki, in his essay on Turgenev and Schopenhauer, treats both "Journey into the Woodland" and "Enough" as central texts for an understanding of the philosopher's influence on Turgenev. Walicki points to Schopenhauer's reconciliation of "two images of nature," and suggests that these two images inform Turgenev's own famous typology of human character in the essay on Hamlet and Don Quixote. My interest here is less in determining the influence of Schopenhauer than in describing the ways in which two visions of nature exist in narrative tension in Turgenev's work. See "Turgenev and Schopenhauer," *Oxford Slavonic Papers* 10 (1962), pp. 1–17.

7. The pastoral oasis is related to the *topos* of the ideal landscape, and figures the "unexpected apparition of a bucolic episode, which breaks the main action or pattern, suspending for a while the heroic, romantic, or pathetic mood of the whole." Rennato Poggioli, *The Oaten Flute* (Cambridge, Mass., 1975), p. 9.

8. H. Gifford briefly notes Turgenev's allusion to Arcadia in his naming of the younger Kirsanov; see "Turgenev" in J.L.I. Fennell, ed., *Nineteenth Century Russian Literature: Studies of Ten Russian Writers* (Berkeley, 1973), p. 157.

9. Poggioli, *The Oaten Flute*, pp. 56–58.

10. N. Gogol', *Sobranie sochinenii*, vol. 2 (Moscow, 1952), p. 9.

11. Edward Crankshaw, *The Shadow of the Winter Palace* (New York, 1976), p. 230.

12. Erwin Panofsky discusses the place of death in the pastoral in his essay "Et in Arcadia Ego" and traces the gradual expulsion of all *memento mori* from the genre. Nonetheless, as Panofsky points out, "the two fundamental tragedies of human existence, frustrated love and death, are by no means absent from Theocritus' *Idylls*." Turgenev's own use of pastoral seems to represent a return to this original, "realist," tradition. Panofsky's essay is found in *Pastoral and Romance: Modern Essays in Criticism*, ed. Eleanor Lincoln (Englewood Cliffs, N.J., 1969).

13. Responding to Herzen's letters on the philistinism and decay of the west, Turgenev refused to see the advent of mass culture as a merely European phenomenon: "The *simoom* you speak of blows not only on the west—it extends to us as well." (P, V,

65). The *simoom* to which Turgenev refers metaphorically is a hot, dry, suffocating wind that blows across the Arabian desert.

14. L. V. Pumpianskii, "*Ottsy i deti*. Istoriko-literaturnyi ocherk," in I. S. Turgenev, *Sochineniia*, 6 (Moscow-Leningrad, 1929).

15. "I dreamt of some strange counterpart to Pugachev" (P, IV, 381). I. Al'mi discusses Turgenev's work as a response to Pushkin's Pugachev—rather than to the historical figure—in her essay "Pushkinskaia traditsiia v romane Turgeneva *Ottsy i deti*," in *Pushkinskii sbornik* (Pskov, 1973), pp. 110–28.

16. See Franco Venturi, *Roots of Revolution* (Chicago, 1960), pp. 102–3.

17. V. Dal', *Tolkovyi slovar' zhivogo velikorusskogo iazyka*, vol. 1 (Moscow, 1978), p. 85.

18. M. Bakhtin, in discussing novels that lament the destruction of the idyll, speaks of their "highlighting of *idyllic objects* as objects not severed from the labor that produced them." "Forms of Time and Chronotope in the Novel," in *The Dialogic Imagination*, ed. M. Holquist, trans. M. Holquist and C. Emerson. Both Fenichka's jars of jam and Arkady's nurse's blanket conform to Bakhtin's formulation.

19. The translation of *bessmyslennyi* as "vacant" is from the Rosemary Edmonds translation, published by Penguin (New York, 1972), p. 102; "absurd" is the term used by Isabel Hapgood (New York, 1907) p. 52. Both Bernard Guerney and Constance Garnett use the term "meaningless," Guerney with the prefatory "well-nigh" and Garnett with the adverb "almost."

20. See the manuscript variants appended to the Academy edition; VIII, 459.

21. The storm that greeted *On the Eve* is suggestive of this—see above, chapter 4, note 2.

22. Poggioli, *The Oaten Flute*, p. 11. See also his discussion of the hunter: "[The shepherd] never confronts the true wild, and this is why he never becomes even a part-time hunter. Venatical attitudes consistently oppose the pastoral . . ." (p. 7).

23. Turgenev's most extensive use of the conventions associated with this figure is in *Spring Torrents*—where Marya Nikolaevna is depicted as Dido, the seductress of Aeneas (XI, 147–48). His first essay to depict such a woman is his unfinished play, "The Temptation of Saint Anthony" (1842), which is an explicit imitation of Merimée's *La Femme est un Diable*. Turgenev thus makes his own contributions to what Mario Praz discusses as the

tradition of La Belle Dame sans Merci; see *The Romantic Agony* (Oxford, 1970), pp. 197–282. E. Kagan-Kans discusses Turgenev's use of the type in *Hamlet and Don-Quixote: Turgenev's Ambivalent Vision* (The Hague, 1975), pp. 41–56.

24. Turgenev kept a diary in Bazarov's name that he subsequently destroyed. Cf. *"On Fathers and Children"*: "During the whole period of writing I felt an involuntary attraction to him" (XIV, 99).

25. A. I. Batiuto points to the Pascalian subtexts of this speech; Bazarov is echoing Pascal's "man without faith" from the *Pensées*. *Turgenev-romanist* (Leningrad, 1972), pp. 60–65.

26. Ovid, *The Metamorphoses*, bk. III; trans. R. Humphries (Bloomington, Ind., 1955), pp. 61–64.

27. The version of the Actaeon story told by Hyginus reads the encounter more explicitly than does Ovid: "Actaeon, son of Aristaeus and Autonoe, a shepherd, saw Diana bathing and desired to ravish her. Angry at this, Diana made horns grow on his head, and he was devoured by his own dogs." The translation is by Mary Grant, *Myths of Hyginus* (Kansas University, 1960), p. 139. For a discussion of the representation and significance of rape throughout the *Metamorphoses* see Leo C. Curran, "Rape and Rape Victims in *The Metamorphoses*" in J. Peradotto and J. P. Sullivan, eds., *Women in the Ancient World: The Arethusa Papers* (Albany, N.Y., 1984), pp. 263–86.

28. Fenichka sits in the arbor with a pile of dew-laden roses: Bazarov's flirtation with her uses the classic vocabulary of pastoral seduction, where the rose stands for the innocent beauty the lover desires. Ronsard's poems on this topic are perhaps the most famous; Turgenev himself wrote a poem based on these conventions as a young man, "The Blossom" (*"Tsvetok"*) (I, 29).

29. The phrase is Mary Grant's, *Myths of Hyginus*.

30. Merezhkovskii, "Turgenev," p. 58.

Conclusion

1. T. S. Eliot, "Turgenev," in *The Egoist* (December 1917), p. 167.

BIBLIOGRAPHY

Al'mi, I. "Pushkinskaia traditsiia v romane Turgeneva *Ottsy i deti.*" In *Pushkinskii sbornik*, pp. 110–28. Pskov, 1973.

Baevskii, V. "*Rudin* I. S. Turgeneva (k voprosu o zhanre)." *Voprosy literatury*, No. 2, (1958), pp. 134–38.

Bakhmetov, ed. *Izbrannye zhitiia sviatykh, kratko izlozhennye.* . . . Moscow, 1958.

Bakhtin, M. M. "Avtor i geroi v èsteticheskoi deiatel'nosti." In *Èstetika slovesnogo tvorchestva*, pp. 9–191. Moscow, 1986.

———. "Forms of Time and Chronotope in the Novel." In *The Dialogic Imagination*, ed. M. Holquist, trans. M. Holquist and C. Emerson, pp. 84–258. Austin, Texas, 1981.

Batiuto, A. I. "Svoeobrazie romanov Turgeneva 50–x nachala 60–kh godov." In *Problemy realizma russkoi literatury XIX veka*, pp. 133–61. Moscow-Leningrad, 1961.

———. *Turgenev—romanist.* Leningrad, 1972.

Bialyi, G. *Turgenev i russkii realizm.* Moscow-Leningrad, 1962.

Booth, W. *The Rhetoric of Fiction.* Chicago, 1961.

Brodskii, N. L. "Bakunin i Rudin." *Katorga i ssylka*, no. 5. Moscow, 1926.

———. "Genealogiia romana *Rudin.*" In *Pamiati P. N. Sakulina*, pp. 18–35. Moscow, 1931.

———. "Khudozhniki slova o Turgeneve." In *Turgenev i ego vremeni*. Moscow-Petrograd, 1923.

Brooks, Peter. *The Melodramatic Imagination.* New York, 1985.

———. *Reading for the Plot.* New York, 1984.

Chernyshevskii, N. G. "Russkii chelovek na rendez-vous." *Polnoe sobranie sochinenii v 15-i tomakh*, vol. 5. Moscow, 1939–53.

Chmielewski, E. *Tribune of the Slavophiles.* University of Florida Press, 1962.

Costlow, Jane T. "The Death of Rhetoric in *Rudin.*" *Russian Literature*, 16 (1984), pp. 375–84.

Crankshaw, E. *The Shadow of the Winter Palace.* New York, 1976.

Curran, L. C."Rape and Rape Victims in *The Metamorphoses.*" In *Women in the Ancient World: The Arethusa Papers*, ed. J. Peradotto and J. P. Sullivan, pp. 264–86. Albany, N.Y., 1984.

Dal', V. *Tolkovyi slovar' zhivogo velikorusskogo iazyka.* Moscow, 1978.

Dostoevskii, F. M. "O liubvi k narodu." In *F. M. Dostoevskii ob iskusstve,* pp. 455–56. Moscow, 1973.

Droblenkova, N. F. " 'Zhivye Moshchi' Turgeneva." In *Turgenevskii sbornik,* 5, pp. 289–302. Leningrad, 1969.

Egunov, A. N. " 'Veshnie vody.' Latinskie ssylki v povesti Turgeneva." In *Turgenevskii sbornik,* 4, pp. 182–89. Leningrad, 1968.

Eikhenbaum, B. *Lev Tolstoi.* Leningrad, 1928–31.

Eliot, T. S. "Turgenev." In *The Egoist* (December 1917), p. 167.

Ellis, John M. *The Theory of Literary Criticism: A Logical Analysis.* Berkeley, 1974.

Empson, W. *Some Versions of Pastoral.* New York, 1974.

Freeborne, R. *Turgenev: The Novelist's Novelist.* London, 1960.

Gabel', M. O. "Tvorcheskaia istoriia romana *Rudin.*" *Literaturnoe nasledstvo* 76 (1967), pp. 9–70.

Gershenzon, M. *Mechta i mysl' I. S. Turgeneva.* Providence, R.I., 1970.

Gertsen, A. I. *Sobranie sochinenii v vos'mi tomakh.* Moscow, 1975.

Gifford, H. "Turgenev." In *Nineteenth-Century Russian Literature: Studies of Ten Russian Writers,* ed. J.L.I. Fennell, pp. 143–67, Berkeley, 1973.

Gogol', N. *Sobranie sochinenii.* Moscow, 1952.

Granjard, H. *Ivan Tourguénev et les courants politiques et sociaux de son temps.* Paris, 1966.

Grant, M., trans. *Myths of Hyginus.* University of Kansas Press, 1960.

Grigor'ev, A. "Moe znakomstvo s Vitalinym." *Repertuar i panteon* (1845), 11:8.

Gustafson, R. *The Imagination of Spring: The Poetry of Afanasy Fet.* New Haven, Conn., 1966.

Heilbrun, C. *Toward a Recognition of Androgyny.* New York, 1982.

Hellgren, L. *Dialogue in Turgenev's Novels: Speech Introductory Devices.* Stockholm, 1980.

Hippisley, A. R. "The Emblem in Russian Literature." *Russian Literature* 16 (1984), pp. 289–304.

Holquist, M. J. "The Gaps in Christology: *The Idiot.*" In *Dostoevsky and the Novel,* pp. 102-23. Evanston, Ill., 1977.

Hubbs, J. "The Worship of Mother Earth in Russian Culture." In

Mother Worship, ed. J. P. Preston, pp. 123–44. Chapel Hill, N.C., 1982.

Iezuitova, R. V. "Svetskaia povest'." In *Russkaia povest' XIX v.*, ed. B. S. Meilakh, pp. 169–99. Leningrad, 1973.

Ingham, N. "Turgenev in the Garden." *Mnemozina* (1974).

Jackson, R. L. "The Root and the Flower. Dostoevsky and Turgenev: A Comparative Esthetic." *Yale Review* (Winter 1974), pp. 228–50.

———. "The Turgenev Question." *Sewanee Review* 93 (1985), pp. 300–309.

Jakobson, R. "Two Aspects of Language and Two Types of Aphasic Disturbances." In *Fundamentals of Language*, pp. 69–96. The Hague, 1971.

James, H. *Literary Criticism*. Vol. 2. New York, 1984.

James, W. *The Letters of William James*. Ed. H. James. Boston, 1920.

Jung, C. G. *Memories, Dreams, Reflections*. New York, 1965.

Kagan-Kans, E. *Hamlet and Don-Quixote: Turgenev's Ambivalent Vision*. The Hague, 1975.

Kermode, F. *The Genesis of Secrecy: On the Interpretation of Narrative*. Cambridge, Mass., 1979.

———. *The Sense of an Ending: Studies in the Theory of Fiction*. London, 1966.

Krivocheine, B. *The Ascetic and Theological Teaching of Gregory Palamas*. London, 1954.

Lamartine, Alphonse. *Oeuvres poétiques complètes de Lamartine*. Paris, 1963.

Ledkovsky, M. *The Other Turgenev: From Romanticism to Symbolism*. Wurzburg, 1973.

Lednicki, W. *Bits of Table Talk on Pushkin, Michiewicz, Goethe, Turgenev and Sienkiewicz*. The Hague, 1956.

Lotman, Iu. *Stat'i po tipologii kultury*. Tartu, 1970.

Lotman, L. M. "Turgenev i Fet." In *Turgenev i ego sovremenniki*. Leningrad, 1977.

Markovich, V. M. *I. S. Turgenev i russkii realisticheskii roman*. Leningrad, 1982.

Merezhkovskii, D. "Turgenev." In *Polnoe sobranie sochinenii*, vol. 17. Moscow, 1914.

Miliukov, P. *Iz istorii russkoi intelligentsii*. St. Petersburg, 1903.

Muchnic, H. *An Introduction to Russian Literature*. New York, 1964.

Orlovskii, S. *Lirika molodogo Turgeneva.* Prague, 1926.

Ovid. *The Metamorphoses.* Trans. R. Humphries. Bloomington, Ind., 1955.

Panofsky, E. "Et in Arcadia Ego." In *Pastoral and Romance: Modern Essays in Criticism,* ed. E. Lincoln. Englewood Cliffs, N.J., 1969.

Peterson, D. *The Clement Vision: Poetic Realism in Turgenev and James.* Port Washington, N.Y., 1975.

Pisarev, D. *Literaturnaia kritika v trekh tomakh.* Leningrad, 1981.

Poggioli, R. *The Oaten Flute.* Cambridge, Mass., 1975.

Praz, M. *The Romantic Agony.* Oxford, 1970.

Pumpianskii, L. V: "Ottsy i deti. Istoriko-literaturnyi ocherk." In *I. S. Turgenev: Materialy i issledovaniia,* ed. N. L. Brodskii. Orel, 1940.

Shatalov, S. *Khudozhestvennyi mir I. S. Turgeneva.* Moscow, 1979.

———. *Problemy poetiki I. S. Turgeneva.* Moscow, 1969.

Spacks, P. M. *Gossip.* New York, 1985.

Tanner, T. *Adultery in the Novel.* Baltimore, 1979.

I. S. Turgenev v vospominaniiakh sovremennikov. Moscow, 1983.

Turgenev, I. S. *Polnoe sobranie sochinenii i pisem v dvadtsati vos'mi tomakh.* Moscow, 1960–68.

———. *Sochineniia.* Moscow-Leningrad, 1929.

Venturi, F. *Roots of Revolution.* Chicago, 1960.

Virgil. *The Aeneid.* Trans. R. Fitzgerald. New York, 1980.

Walicki, A. "Turgenev and Schopenhauer." *Oxford Slavonic Papers* 10 (1962), pp. 1–17.

INDEX

DATE DUE

AUG - 8 1997	
MAR - 9 2000	